CONTENT
MARKETING,
ENGINEERED

CONTENT MARKETING, ENGINEERED

Build Trust and Convert Buyers—
——with Technical Content

WENDY COVEY

RIVER GROVE
BOOKS

Published by River Grove Books
Austin, TX
www.rivergrovebooks.com

Distributed by River Grove Books
Cover design by Laura Lee Daigle
Publisher's Cataloging-in-Publication data is available.

Print ISBN: 978-1-63299-285-7

eBook ISBN: 978-1-63299-286-4

First Edition

Advance Praise for
Content Marketing, Engineered

"For the last decade, Wendy has helped technical B2B companies successfully implement marketing programs that impact the bottom line. She understands the important nuances needed to develop content that really connects with engineering buyers. This book is a valuable and practical guide for organizations looking to start or strengthen their marketing efforts with a clear, content-based approach that's executable and measurable."

—**Eric Starkloff**, CEO, National Instruments

"When you're selling technical solutions, it's critical that your marketing expertise comes from someone who knows the nuances of your audience. Wendy and her team at TREW Marketing used the content-based framework outlined in this book to help us implement an inbound marketing approach fueled by quality technical content. Through this methodology we've consistently generated technical leads and built trust with prospects, helping Vertech to grow our business."

—**Titus Crabb**, President, Vertech Industrial Systems

"The digital transformation of industry, known as Industry 4.0, IoT, IIoT, and smart manufacturing impacts manufacturers, suppliers, and industrial system integrators. These technical audiences have the opportunity to better understand their markets and position solutions to meet the emerging needs of their clients and prospects. From a marketing perspective, this requires significant work to develop an offer with a clear foundation of the company's brand and associated value proposition. Wendy Covey's extensive background with engineering-centric companies makes her an authority in the field, and she's captured her expertise in this book to help you define and target your market with planned, measurable content and offers."

—**Jose Rivera**, CEO, Control System Integrators Association

"Wendy delivers practical guidance for middle-market companies looking to grow their business through content marketing. The presentations and workshops delivered by her and the TREW team helped to fuel sustained channel partner growth at ANSYS—this book now makes the same critical information accessible to companies across the globe."

— **Josh Doty**, Global Partner Director, ANSYS

To my husband, Randy

Thank you for inspiring me to tackle new adventures,
to never sit still, and be a better me.

Randy introduced the love of
fishing to our family

Randy has great patience with
me and my decade-long bragging
spree about this record redfish

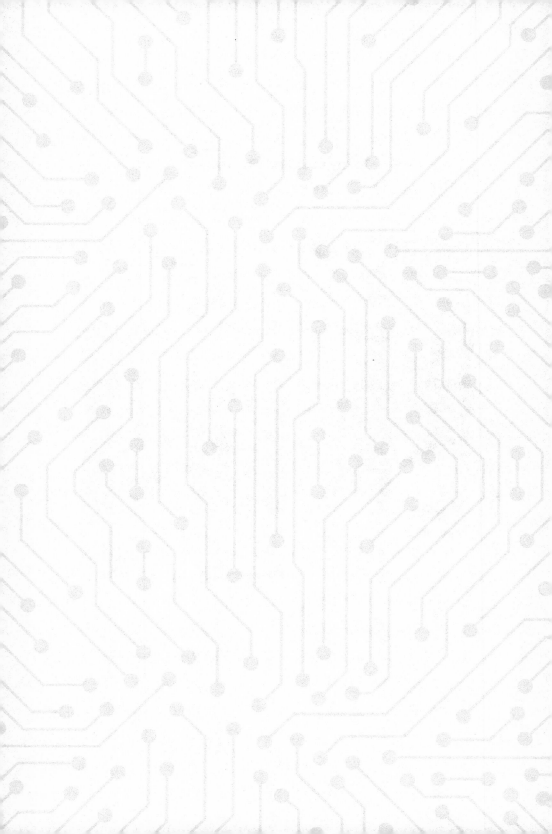

Contents

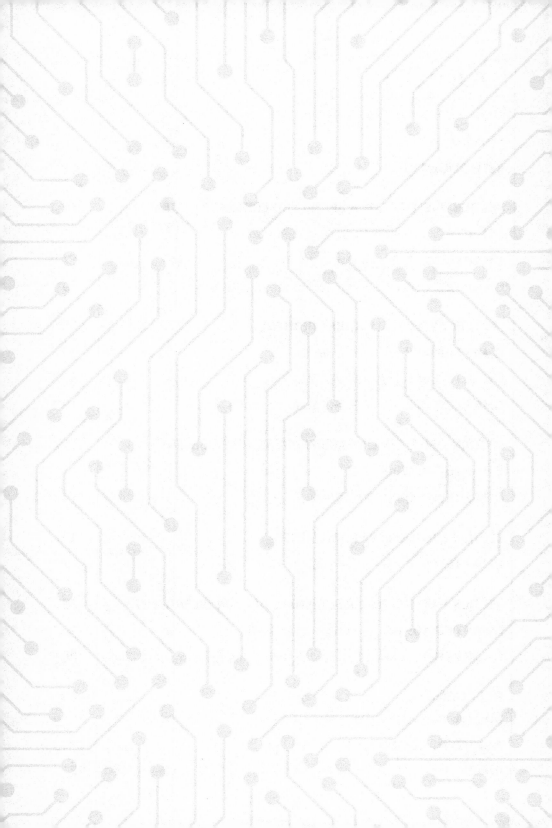

Foreword

JD Sherman
*HubSpot Chief
Operating Officer*

My background is in finance for the cloud computing and semiconductor businesses, but here I am, advocating for a marketing book. Let me tell you why: Before serving as the president and COO of HubSpot, I was a CFO. Given the nature of that role, I cared immensely about ROI and growing profitability. Marketing was, frankly, just another expense line item to me. As a COO, I still care about ROI and growth, but I've come to understand how inbound marketing can create an asset that helps drive business growth. That's part of HubSpot's mission: We're passionate about uniting software, education, and community to help businesses grow better every day.

The way people live, work, shop, and buy has changed dramatically. We're so much harder to interrupt with traditional marketing and advertising. Not only that, but we absolutely hate being interrupted! When we are, the brands responsible suffer in our eyes, and we have a voice to share how we feel via social media. Successful inbound marketing hinges on creating compelling content that customers are drawn to and that matches the way they live, work, shop, and buy today.

But, like all great things, inbound marketing takes time and commitment. There are plans to make, obstacles to overcome, and work to be done in order to reap the trust and leads that come from content.

The early days of inbound marketing consisted of simply shifting some printed mailer spending to content that would be findable via internet search. Now, inbound marketing is about talking to customers in their languages. We've learned that the more you know your buyers, the better you can tailor your content marketing plans and messaging to them. Marketers must extensively know the ins and outs of their specific buyer personas—factors like their biggest headaches, their roles in a purchase decision, and their criteria for a successful solution. And marketers must add value for specific personas with smart, helpful content before they can expect to extract value via a sales engagement.

At HubSpot, we've found that great content compounds in value, growing in returns over time. In my CFO parlance, you're creating a valuable asset with your content rather than renting someone else's asset with traditional advertising. It might seem odd to compare marketing to manufacturing, but it's actually a pretty good analogy! In many ways, you're building a "factory" with your content. If you make a plan to build a factory to produce widgets, you don't produce a single widget during the planning phase or even the building phase. You're investing time, money, and energy, and it's all an expense. But the day that factory is complete, it's an asset. You're optimizing and tweaking the widget and production line, and that factory is making widgets even while you sleep. Much like that factory, publishing a few blog posts won't change your business today, but a steady stream of content targeted for your audience over time will produce results. Here at HubSpot, we see that 90 percent or more of our site traffic comes from content created months ago rather than the content we just released. By nurturing that traffic with fresh and targeted content and offers, we create users of our software, leads for our sales team, and ultimately customers.

This is where Wendy Covey comes in. Wendy has spent her career marketing to technical audiences. Most recently, she's spent more than a decade leading TREW Marketing, an agency specializing in marketing to those engineers. Wendy and her team have entrenched themselves in the nuanced language and details of the engineer, and they've built their business through a long-standing commitment to creating technical content that converts. Seeing the success TREW Marketing produces for their technical clients, we invited Wendy to the HubSpot Partner Advisory Council years ago. She's been a valuable asset to us ever since as we hone and refine our platform to help customers grow their businesses through targeted persona relationships and compelling content.

Everything Wendy tells you in this book—everything she tells clients—TREW Marketing has done in its own content marketing. Wendy's advice is built on years of research and experience honing content marketing plans for a targeted, technical audience. Read this book, and then go and do. Build your factory so you can create those visits and leads while you sleep.

—JD Sherman
HubSpot Chief Operating Officer

Introduction

In high school, my electrical-engineer brother used to take apart broken televisions discarded by neighbors during bulk trash pickup, fix them, and leave them like new on the front steps of their original owners. Now he works with a team of network engineers to determine communications configurations for far-flung military encampments, ensuring our soldiers stay in close contact with base camp and beyond. He can be annoyingly detail-oriented, calling me out on illogical reasoning—which was quite irritating as a teenage girl—but I truly appreciate the different way he thinks, processes information, and makes decisions. (And he would not have worn Mork & Mindy rainbow suspenders!)

Chances are if you've picked up this book, you fall into one of two camps: you're a marketer focused on reaching engineers or an engineer learning to become a marketer. In both cases, you've chosen a unique profession, because an engineer (and a like-minded technical buyer) doesn't behave the same as your typical B2B buyer. To successfully reach these audiences, you need a greatly differentiated approach.

Engineers are inventors, complex problem solvers, and technology drivers. Their work makes a significant impact on our everyday lives, from the drinking water that sustains us to the digital devices we love to the vehicle airbags that keep us safe. Think about the engineers you know in your life. They are likely trustworthy, analytical, logical, and creative. Does this description fit?

When facing complex challenges that often pose significant risks if not addressed correctly, engineers seek out information from trusted sources. Who and what are these sources, and how does the engineer know they can be trusted?

Traditionally, a company's technical sales force was its primary source of information, and a company brochure or catalog was the core piece of reference content for a purchase decision. Salespeople would visit (hopefully invited) or "dial for dollars" to connect with their target buyers.

Today's engineer buyers are in charge of their interactions with your company. Interruptive sales solicitations and physical meet-and-greet activities have been replaced. The seminar has given way to the webinar; the trade show pendulum has swung towards an always-on search engine or industry directory; and the early-stage sales visit, if there is one at all, starts with an online chat.

Instead of sales holding information hostage, engineers can find the content they need online. They expect to conduct a great deal of independent research before engaging with vendors. Companies who share expertise through quality content on a consistent basis are seen as trusted resources, spend less per lead, and achieve greater pipeline efficiency.

Gaining the trust of an engineer is not an easy task. They can tell the difference between material generated by a non-technical marketing coordinator working in a silo versus content produced by a subject-matter expert. Producing smart, timely, and accurate technical content is essential to build trust and win business with technical professionals.

So, if content generosity builds trust, what does trust do for your business? A recent study of technical B2B services companies showed that those who've invested in establishing and maintaining a strong brand positively affect customers' purchase and repurchase decisions. These strong-branded companies generated greater revenue and cash flow stability than their non-branded counterparts, resulting in shareholders attaching significant economic net value to B2B service brands. This data is a call to action for owners planning to tango with an equity firm as part of their growth or exit plan.

The 2019 TREW Marketing and IEEE Smart Marketing for Engineers research findings show that 90 percent of engineers are more likely to do business with a company that regularly produces new or updated content.

And here's more good news: Unlike many other marketing activities, such as a trade show booth that is torn down at the end of the event or search advertising that concludes the second you stop paying, content lives on indefinitely. You must make an up-front investment to create your content marketing foundation, but with regular optimization and promotion your content will generate new interest and leads for years to come at a bargain lifetime cost per lead.

How to Use This Book

This book guides you through the key steps in gaining awareness and building trust with technical buyers using compelling content. This content is thoughtfully constructed to inform, educate, and help your buyer through their journey to purchase and beyond. By the time you reach the last page of this book, you'll know the entire end-to-end content marketing process, from planning and writing to publishing, promoting, and measuring.

Note that throughout the book you'll see suggestions on when to request insight from executive teams, opinions from sales, or expertise from subject-matter experts (SMEs) in your organization. Take the time to leverage these people. Looping them in will not only get you the information you need but also help you educate them on marketing and its value. This ultimately creates informed champions across your organization who can help support marketing in the years to come.

Section One of this book starts with identifying and defining your audience personas. This was a purposeful choice because all content should be written, published, and promoted with these personas in mind. After that, you'll learn why strong brands make a powerful impact on your business performance and market perception and discover how to construct your company story.

Then, you'll learn each key step of developing a comprehensive content plan, from cross-functional teamwork and goal-setting to creating topic clusters and selecting content form factors.

Writing for technical audiences can be a tough job without having an established process, healthy collaboration with SMEs, and thoughtful consideration about the target persona. Section Two guides you through these critical success factors, breaks down the best practices of content creation by content type, flags common grammatical errors, and offers tips on choosing imagery.

You'll then be immersed in the ins and outs of content publishing and promoting with a hefty focus on web, search optimization, and inbound marketing channels. You'll learn the importance of marketing technology for your content marketing efforts. Certain types of web pages, such as pillar pages, blogs, and landing pages, make a huge impact on web usability and on-page SEO. By the time you reach the end of the publishing section, you'll know how to develop and optimize each kind of web page following best practices.

Next, you'll dive into multichannel content promotion, including multiple research findings to help guide budgetary allocation decisions. This chapter will give you a deep understanding of when to use each channel within your content promotion plans and provide you with best practices for tactical activity.

Sales will be a big consumer of your content, in addition to your prospects. Are you creating what they need? In chapter 9, you'll learn some of the latest and most popular sales-oriented content form factors and how to create them.

Next, you'll learn which key metrics and industry benchmarks gauge whether your content marketing initiatives are working. Included are both high-level indicators and detailed troubleshooting tips for when your metrics don't look so hot.

The final chapter inspires you to take action. Included are real-world statistics on content marketing return on investment (ROI), advice on expected time to results, and helpful tips for starting and building upon your present state.

By consistently creating quality content, and thoughtfully positioning and promoting this content, you will become a trusted resource for engineers. Buyers will more easily find your website, self-select as qualified leads, and engage with sales. Your sales reps will find themselves less reliant on outbound lead sourcing and more likely to act as advisers to continue a buyer's educational journey. All of this effort translates to growth for your business.

I hope that in the following pages, you'll find inspiration and direct, practical advice for working smarter on your own marketing journey.

—Wendy Covey

Section One

Develop a Brand and Content Strategy

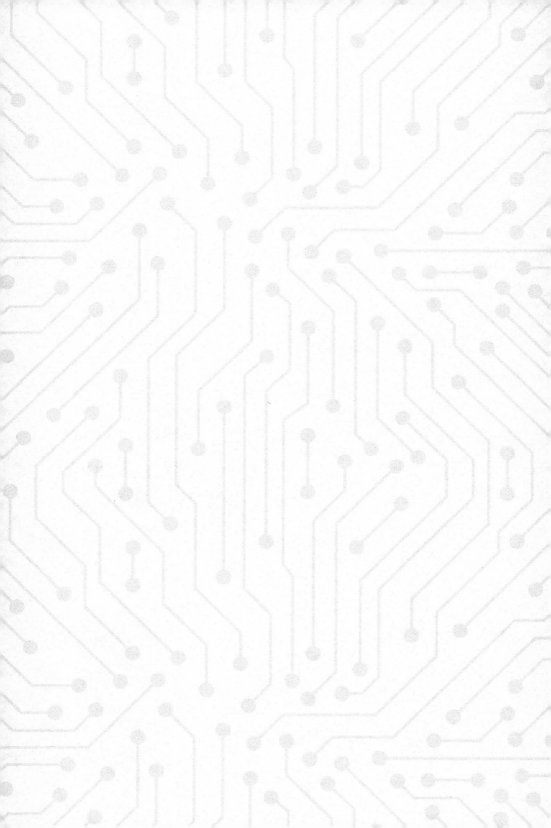

Chapter 1
DEFINE AUDIENCE PERSONAS

Your brand is your company's narrative. It describes the problems your customers face, guides them to the solutions you provide, and shows the results your solutions deliver. Your brand then becomes the backbone of your content strategy.

It's easy to make your brand story all about you and your products or services, but successful brands make their customers the focus. Brand development starts with deeply knowing your customers and then moves on to positioning your company, developing core messages, and telling stories. Once you know the narrative you're sharing and who you're sharing it with, you can set objectives and key performance indicators (KPIs), evaluate content topics and types, and create a content plan to reach your audience with your message.

Whether your company is a startup with one solution or a multimillion-dollar enterprise with a diverse client base, it's smart to break down the pool of potential customers beyond prioritized audience segments and into buyer personas. By defining and utilizing personas, you can anticipate the needs of prospects and cater your content to address their needs and concerns.

What Are Personas?

Buyer personas are fictional representations of your ideal customers based on demographic data, online behavior, and your educated speculation about personal histories, motivations, and concerns.

For example, you may define one of your personas as "VP of Engineering Val," a business executive who cares most about cost and long-term support. A second persona could be "Engineer Evan," an engineering manager or senior staff engineer who is an expert in your technology

area and wants to do a deep dive into the
technical capabilities of your product or
how you deliver a service. Evan greatly
influences Val, but Val makes the final
decisions. Val and Evan have very different concerns. They want various types
of information about your company and
product, and they go to different places to
find that information.

> **With a persona-based approach, your content has a greater impact on your prospects and increases your marketing efficiency.**

By walking through the exercise
of understanding your personas, such
as Val and Evan, you can apply faces,
personalities, job descriptions, and key
elements of the buying decision to each and better customize your
website and marketing efforts, from messaging to content selection.
With a persona-based approach, your content has a greater impact on
your prospects and increases your marketing efficiency.

Brainstorm and Prioritize Personas

The first step in creating buyer personas is to brainstorm the four types
of personas:

- **Decision Makers**: Those making the final decision on which
  product or service to purchase; often C-level roles or VPs of
  engineering, sales, or product. Typical decision-maker personas
  place a high value on ROI.
- **Influencers**: Those tasked with vetting purchase options and presenting final recommendations to a decision maker; often engineering, product, project, or technical managers. They care most
  about meeting the business goals they're tasked with on time and
  within budget; they may also care about technical specs, downtime, and overall reliability or maintenance.

- **Buyers**: Those completing purchases; often procurement. They care most about cost and contract details.
- **End Users**: Those using your final product or solution; often application engineers or IT. They care most about how the product actually works and helps them get their jobs done.

Note that titles for each persona type vary greatly by company size (for example, a decision maker at a $500M company may be a manager but at a $5M company could be a CEO) or organizational structure (an influencer vetting solution options may also be the end user who will use it).

Involve multiple members of your team in this discussion. Sales is particularly important because they work with these personas daily. Get their insight on the most critical personas for your company and focus on the personas that represent the best customers for your organization.

To develop a comprehensive list of possible personas, ask your internal team of sales and project managers to think of the typical buying process for your customers and discuss the answers to the following:

- Who do you first engage with?
- Who influences that person?
- Who makes the final decision?

Are your personas different across industries, product lines, service types, or company size?

Once you have your full list, identify the personas that have similar needs or roles and consider merging them. From here, prioritize your list of personas by considering their impact on the final purchase decision, their relationship to your company, and the size of the audience persona group.

For example, if a key influencer group has only a few members, you may decide it's best for sales to own those relationships and not have marketing prioritize them as a larger group. Small- and middle-market companies typically have the bandwidth to focus on three to five primary personas, particularly when just starting this type of marketing approach. Larger companies may simultaneously balance fifteen or more personas among their various product or solution divisions.

Create Personas

Once you've finished brainstorming and prioritizing, you need to create your actual personas. Start with the top three personas: those who are most likely to bring you in or influence the sale. This can be one decision maker and two influencers who have specific needs based on their industry, or a decision maker, an influencer, and an end user who need nurturing and support to succeed with your product or service and repurchase it later.

Begin this process by asking yourself and your team the following questions to understand **where to reach** each persona and pinpoint the tone and style of marketing that speak most clearly to the customers who fit each persona:

- What are their job roles and titles?
- What are their levels of responsibility (business, system, product, etc.)?
- What are their levels of budget authority?
- What degree(s) do they hold?

To understand the **key messages and content** relevant to each persona, ask:

- What are their biggest pain points?
- What does success look like in their roles? What are their goals?
- How do you help them reach these goals?
- What are their objections to working with you?

To identify the **key marketing activities** that resonate with each persona, ask:

- How do they learn about new information for their jobs?
- What publications do they read? What trade shows do they attend?
- What terms are they searching for?
- What career-based associations or social networks do they belong to?

Give each persona a name, like "Sales Manager Sam" or "Technical Tim," and add a photo to the documents to define the personas. The photo may not seem necessary, but it's helpful for your team to be able to visualize each persona. Consider naming or modeling your persona after an actual customer that your team knows to help them relate to the persona.

Your team will often have very distinct images of each customer persona: They are highly risk averse; they're introverted; they are budget-driven; they conduct business through their relationships. If you modeled the persona after a customer your team knows, you may want to choose a photo showing that actual person. Or you may want to find a representative image of your persona at work to give context to their environment. Keep debating until you find a picture that captures the consensus of your team; take the time to get the photo right, so internally you can easily reference the personas.

These names, definitions, and images will help your team quickly reference which type of prospect you're talking about when a new opportunity arises. Imagine being able to make a comment such as, "That person was a total Sam," and all your team members nod their heads in understanding. Later, when you're creating content, you'll look back at these personas and develop content with messages and solutions precisely designed to meet a specific persona's needs. Once you've gained traction with persona-based marketing activities for your top three personas, add more and further refine over time.

Persona Example

The best way to explain personas is to use examples. Let's talk about Oil/Gas Engineer Ethan.

Looking at Oil/Gas Engineer Ethan, you can see he's a well-respected, senior engineer in his firm with superior academic and field credentials. He is the go-to guy inside his Fortune 1000 company for opinions on adopting new technologies. When Ethan is researching his products, he goes first to the specifications to determine the requirements for integrating new technology into an existing system. In the energy sector, existing systems can live in very remote, rugged areas such as on the ocean floor or in desert terrain, and they are very expensive to maintain, so Ethan is thorough in his research.

He reads all the technical information he can and seeks out quality and test/trial data to see proof of real-world performance. He must be convinced that the product is proven and reliable before he ever meets with a technical counterpart at the supplier. He has no room for error in his applications, and his reputation is on the line with each decision he makes.

"I research new technologies that are proven, reliable, and compatible with our existing systems. Company leaders and my engineering peers rely on my technical opinion, so I am analytical and meticulous in my due diligence. I enjoy working with technology and the engineers who create it, especially when I find an innovative new partner who has promising technology and is trustworthy and technically competent. I keep up by reading technical journals and talking with my cohorts in the industry at technical conferences and symposiums."

OIL/GAS ENGINEER ETHAN

Age: 40-50
Gender: Mostly Male
Degree: Master's or Doctorate Degree in Engineering
Job Title: Senior-Level Engineer, System Engineer
Experience Level: 20+ Years
Industry: Oil/Gas Exploration

IDENTIFIERS

- Works on manufacturing and engineering processes
- Regularly evaluates technologies to assess their potential for meeting his needs
- Stays abreast of new technologies and serves as an internal technology expert/consultant

GOALS

- Getting the right solution the first time
- Easily integrating new technology into his current system
- Minimizing risk (downtime and accidents)

PREFERENCES

Communication Preference: Email
Social Media Channels: LinkedIn
How They Find You: Google, Publications (Oil & Gas Journal, World Oil, Hydrocarbon Processing), Peers
Tradeshows They Attend: Upstream Onshore Oil & Gas, Offshore Technology Conference

CHALLENGES

- Top concern is system reliability
- Secondary concern is finding the best, most reliable new technology
- Cost is a concern only in a few corner application areas

WHAT WE CAN DO:

- Detailed and extensive field and lab testing, third-party testing, reliably proven specs
- Face-to-face meetings, eye contact, high morale
- Proven expertise

Ethan is well known in his tight-knit community of energy technologists, and he gets most of his information from technical conferences, leading academicians, and peers he trusts.

One last element of persona development to consider is where the persona is in the technology adoption life cycle. This model for high-tech marketing was made famous by Geoffrey Moore in his book *Crossing the Chasm.*

As you can imagine, customer personas can vary widely with differences in educational levels, pain points, concerns, preferred information sources, and risk level. By defining these and other elements and finding the right persona photo, you are ready to segment your messaging, plan your content development, and decide on the optimal marketing approach to reach each specific persona.

Customer Voice

Understanding your customers will help inform your personas. Consider reaching out to key customers to gather data on exactly who they are, what motivates them, and how they define success. Example customer interview questions:

- What initial challenges drove you to search for a new solution?
- Who or what supplied the data you needed to inform your decision?
- How did you decide which company to work with?
- What were the key factors for a successful solution?
- Why do you continue to work with our team?
- What type of information helps you be successful at your job?

Take the Next Step with Personas

The more information you have about your buyer, the more effective you can be in marketing to them. Once you're comfortable with your personas and have been successfully marketing to them, consider refining them further with a qualitative research project centered around customer interviews.

Customer interviews are different from traditional research in the sense that the approach is more flexible and each conversation is different. By analyzing the qualitative data from the interviews, you can more precisely define persona elements such as job roles represented on customer buying teams, the point when decisions transition from an influencer to a decision maker, triggers that lead buyers to begin searching for solutions, and the outcomes or benefits they expect from their purchases. Having this kind of information strengthens content planning, message creation, and sales materials development. During those interviews, you may uncover opportunities to create case studies or pass along feedback to your product or services development team. This is a great side benefit of customer interviews, but case studies shouldn't be the primary focus of your interview.

You can start your in-depth research by focusing on one persona. Identify ten to fifteen customers who match the persona and who would be willing to be interviewed for up to thirty minutes. Then create an interview script with questions to dive deeper into the customers' job roles, pains, and buying processes. After interviews are complete, define themes and consider creating an overview of the top five to ten findings for your sales, marketing, and leadership teams.

Personas are a critical part of catering your content to your audience, and the best way to keep your content current and relevant to your audience is to keep your personas current. Just as your company grows and offers new products and services, your personas should grow and develop. Once a year, be sure to review your personas with your marketing, sales, and service delivery teams. As you spend more time with clients, you'll notice new things about them and better learn which types of content help influence their buyer's journeys.

Chapter 2
TELL YOUR COMPANY STORY

Though marketing practices change and provide new ways to drive awareness and efficiency, buyers still want authentic messaging from brands they can trust. A compelling brand message backed by great products or services can do wonders for your audience perception and build trust along the way.

Trust, just as in friendships or professional relationships, is built through long-term, consistent communication and interaction with all of your stakeholders, from employees and customers to partners and suppliers.

Gaining the trust of an engineering audience is no easy task. Engineers easily see through a marketing facade that's not technically supported. To win over your technical audience, you need to understand who you are as a company and tell a compelling story about your brand.

Brand Positioning and Messaging Process

Brand positioning is the process of defining your brand. It begins with developing your mission, vision, and core values, and then moves on to creating a company positioning statement. Once these elements are defined, the process moves to messaging a brand tone and attributes and telling your corporate story.

IDENTIFY	DEFINE	WRITE	DEVELOP	CREATE
Customer Problems	Company Mission, Vision, and Core Values	Corporate Positioning Statement	Messaging that Conveys a Strong Brand	Narrative with Storytelling

Key steps in the brand positioning and messaging process.

Brands Create Perception

Brands everywhere have reputations or perceptions that come to mind at the very mention of a company name. Think of brands like Dell, IBM, GM, Intel, Boeing, GE, or Lockheed. Each evokes a perception: the brand is trustworthy, friendly, helpful, deeply technical, reliable, customer oriented, and on the cusp of what's next—or not.

But Who Are You?

If you ask your CEO, your VP of sales, and your VP of research and development to summarize your company, you likely get very different answers, all skewed to the aspect of business in which that person is involved. Through the brand positioning and messaging process, a branding committee interviews stakeholders and strategically defines messaging that represents the company. Here are a few examples of technical companies' final corporate pitches after a complete brand positioning and messaging project.

Silex: "You design and develop it, and Silex Technology will connect it to the network. We transform your products into secure, reliable wireless devices and machines that deliver a completely connected, always-on experience for your customers."

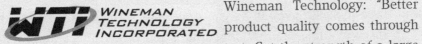

Wineman Technology: "Better product quality comes through test. Get the strength of a large test system development team with deep expertise in a wide range of applications, and the flexibility of a partner nimble enough to listen to your needs and develop a custom solution for your revolutionary technology. With an open architecture and scalable hardware, your test system will advance with your product so you can continue to make insightful, strategic decisions over time."

Hallam-ICS: "When organizations face the demands of growth, competition, regulatory compliance, and legacy equipment in facilities or manufacturing plants, Hallam-ICS is an expert engineering partner that provides proven design, assessment, or commissioning services. Because we understand plant and facility MEP systems, control and automation solutions, and safety implications alike, our engineers design solutions for one area with the other two in mind, producing comprehensive, effective results."

Going step by step through this positioning process leads to a well-thought-out, carefully crafted positioning statement that you can use as the foundation for your website, content, and talking points for your sales team. From a positioning statement, you can create a short elevator pitch that all employees can use to clearly describe your company, the customer problems you solve, and how you are uniquely differentiated from competitors to meet those challenges. With a clear positioning statement in place, you can also create targeted but cohesive messages across business segment and target audiences.

Create a Branding Committee

To develop your brand position, put together a branding committee of about three to seven people. As you draft your company's brand over two to three months, the branding committee should meet weekly to give input and feedback, helping you come to an informed, accurate, and compelling final draft. Depending on your company's size, the committee could include leaders from all or some of the following business areas, along with a marketing director or marketing agency partner:

- Sales for information on customer pains and key concerns
- Product design for information on product features
- Development for insight on product roadmaps and how solutions work
- C-level leaders for the overall vision and direction

Ask your branding committee members to answer the below questions on their own before gathering to discuss their responses. This process allows the group to recognize each person's perspective and helps drive consensus. It is beneficial for not only your brand but also the alignment of your leadership. Ask questions like the following:

- What are your company's goals?
- What are your company's mission and vision?
- What are your core values?
- What are your product or service offerings?
- Who are your clients?
- What makes your company unique?
- How does your current brand differentiate itself from others?
- What do you do better than your competition?
- How does your competition differentiate themselves?
- What makes clients choose your products or services over a competitor's?

Define the Company Mission, Vision, and Core Values

After discussing your branding committee's answers, come to consensus and document your company's mission, vision, and core values. These core elements serve as the foundation for your company's positioning statement. Below are brief definitions and examples to reference while writing yours.

Mission Statement: A brief statement to describe the fundamental purpose of an organization; it rarely changes through the decades.
Examples:

- **Google**: To organize the world's information and make it universally accessible and useful.
- **Nike**: To bring inspiration and innovation to every athlete in the world.
- **Autodesk**: To build software tools to enable people to experience their ideas before they are real.
- **Inte**: To utilize the power of Moore's Law to bring smart, connected devices to every person on earth.
- **National Instruments**: To equip engineers and scientists with systems that accelerate productivity, innovation, and discovery through an open, software-defined platform.
- **Rockwell Automation**: To improve the quality of life by making the world more productive and sustainable.

Vision: This is the long-term dream that states what your company wants to be; it serves as a source of inspiration and is sometimes time-based and updated every ten to fifteen years.
Examples:

- **Tesla**: To create the most compelling car company of the twenty-first century by driving the world's transition to electric vehicles.

- **Google**: To provide access to the world's information in one click.
- **Autodesk**: To help people imagine, design, and create a better world.
- **Intel**: If it's smart and connected, it's best with Intel.
- **Apple**: We believe that we are on the face of the earth to make great products, and that's not changing.

Core Values: These are the fundamental beliefs and expected behaviors of your company.

Examples:

- **Rackspace**: fanatical support; results first; substance over flash; committed to greatness; full disclosure and transparency; passion for our work; treat fellow Rackers like friends and family
- **Keysight Technologies**: high performance; speed and courage; uncompromising integrity and social responsibility
- **ANSYS**: customer focus; results and accountability; innovation; transparency and integrity; mastery, inclusiveness; sense of urgency
- **HubSpot "Culture Code"**: we commit maniacally to both our mission and metrics; we look to the long term and solve for the customer; we share openly and are remarkably transparent; we favor autonomy and take ownership; we believe our best perk is our amazing people; we dare to be different and question the status quo; we recognize that life is short

Write a Corporate Positioning Statement

Next, write your positioning statement. The positioning statement defines your company and audience by identifying your target customer, articulating customer pains, and describing the solutions you deliver. It provides clarification on exactly what you do and how you do it, and it can be used for reference internally. It will become the core foundation for your external messaging.

Elements of a Positioning Statement

Who	Where	Why
Your potential customer's job title, function, decision-making authority, etc.	The industry(ies), region(s), department(s), division(s), etc. of the types of companies where your potential customers work.	Your customer's technical challenges or pain points.

What	How	Unlike
Your solutions, including products, services or overall solutions.	The way you solve your customer's problem, such as processes, tools, service, unique expertise, and best practices.	The drawbacks of alternative approaches such as competitors, using in-house resources, or delaying resolution.

The positioning statement has six core elements, the first three (Who, Where, Why) are about your customers, and the last three (What, How, Unlike) are about your business.

Take a look at an example of a complete positioning statement from a sensors company. Then examine the breakdown of each positioning statement component so you can create your own:

- **Who**: C-level executive, VP of engineering or product, and R&D engineers...

- **Where**: ...in $50-million-plus consumer electronics companies focusing on premium wearable, IoT-enabled devices...

- **Why**: ...looking to gain a competitive advantage with precise sensors that can be integrated seamlessly into very small final devices like watches, heart monitors, or hydration detectors.

- **What**: We create small, unassuming sensors that can collect fifty data points per second and take up only the size of a postage stamp.

- **How**: Our commercial off-the-shelf (COTS) sensors integrate easily into wearable devices and consume minimal power, but our development team can develop custom sensors to meet the specific demands of an application.

- **Unlike**: One-size-fits-all sensors that require engineers to design a product around the sensor, sacrificing look and feel.

Often, teams skip the positioning step and dive right into messaging pitches and differentiators. Don't be that team. Take the time to debate, come to consensus, and document your company or product position before you get to messaging.

Who: Define your customers' jobs or authority. To define the "who," think about your key customers' titles and backgrounds and where they fall in the company's decision-making process.

Examples:

- Directors or managers of R&D, technology, or products
- Engineers and program managers or directors
- Lab managers and their teams
- Technology leaders (engineering managers, VPs, and chief technology officers [CTOs])
- Plant engineers, corporate engineering, and manufacturing operations

Where: Define your customers' companies. To define the "where," think about the types of companies you work with: Are they public or private? Are they regionally located? Do they work in specific industries? Is their size important? What about their stage of business?

Examples:

- Managing test and measurement in validation or production for government and private military and aerospace organizations
- Managing increasing amounts of data in labs
- Building new facilities at manufacturing companies and developing batch process control systems for these facilities
- Working at $100M+, high-growth automotive-based organizations
- Working at Fortune 1000 companies in the chemical, pulp and paper, and power industries

Why: Define your customers' problems. When you're writing your "why," think about challenges from your customers' perspectives. If your company makes sensors, it's easy to rush through the "why" section with "customers who need sensors." And though that's correct, it doesn't get to your customers' key pains and motivations. Dig deeper and explore the answers to these questions: What keeps them up at night? What are they afraid of? What pressures are they getting from management? Answering questions like this helps you define exactly why prospects are looking for solutions. Maybe they need sensors for a medical device, and without the right, custom-designed sensors, they'll never pass the ISO 13485.

Examples:

- Trying to find a partner who can design and integrate sensors into a medical device with proper procedures and documentation for ISO 13485
- Needing to cope with increasingly complex automation systems that must share and report plant floor information to the enterprise
- Looking for a reliable test and measurement system from a proven supplier that can meet stringent time, cost, and technical requirements
- Facing increasingly complex, electronic-embedded systems and seeking solutions that scale with more demanding industry standards
- Needing faster test equipment that is smaller, more energy-efficient, and lower in total cost

What: Define exactly what you do and offer. Describe your solutions and products.

Examples:

- Create COTS products and custom solutions with military-ready, aerospace-quality, scalable specifications

- Provide large-scale plant floor automation, industrial IT, and smart manufacturing solutions that improve overall equipment efficiency (OEE), increase agility, and reduce time to market
- Design and build new, custom test solutions and develop high-volume automated test equipment to your exact specifications
- Provide an ESP product that is a centralized data management platform for tracking samples, processing data, reporting, and managing workflows

How: Define how you specifically meet your customers' challenges. It may be through COTS products, custom software, an extensive design process, specific industry partnerships, or best-in-class support. You may have proprietary IP or regional offices that allow you to service clients directly and immediately. Now is the time to identify exactly how you solve problems.

Examples:

- Customer-first, consultative approach that includes a plan of action incorporating the talent and skill of more than 100 industry professionals who specialize in a range of solutions, from plant floor processes to enterprise systems
- Proven electronic design practices, expert LabVIEW programming, and tailored COTS hardware to help clients design and deliver new products to market
- Expertise tackling the demanding precision of aerospace test that we apply in our manufacturing applications and our high-performance, low-power, modular test equipment with fast delivery

Unlike: Identify your customers' other options if they don't choose you, and note the ramifications of their choices. Other options are typically competitor solutions, DIY and in-house solutions, or no solution (letting their problems go unresolved). Though you may end up using some words, phrases, or even whole sentences from other parts of the positioning statement publicly, the "unlike" section is meant only for internal alignment.

Examples:

- Offshore outsourcing where communication is difficult
- Integrators that lack experience meeting industry challenges and addressing the demands of government contractors and aerospace/defense applications
- Costly, brand-name business consultants who lack real-world experience with plant floor automation systems and manufacturing business processes

Incumbent suppliers that offer only COTS components and over-promise on products labeled "easy-to-use" or underdeliver with solutions that reach obsolescence quickly.

Note that through the positioning process, you'll always be able to think about outliers. You may work with $100 million companies, but you also may have conducted business with a startup in the last year. Push your team to define your *ideal* customers. By critically narrowing down who you're best positioned to work with, you can spend your time marketing to the prospects that will help your business instead of distracting from it.

With your core foundational pieces defined—mission, vision, and core values—and the six elements of the positioning statement created, you are now ready for the final steps in the branding process: harnessing the power of a strong brand and telling your story.

Develop Messaging That Conveys a Strong Brand

Brand perception is what customers—both current and potential—think about you. Brands are established by building trust in a one-of-a-kind promise about who you are, what you stand for, and what unique, meaningful benefits you deliver. You build your brand by living up to your promise every single time people come in contact with your name, your message, or your business, and you strengthen your brand by consistently reinforcing your brand promise. Strong brands come from companies that decide what they want to be, message their brand well, and deliver on their brand promise.

Agree on Brand Attributes and Tone

Brand attributes are what you stand for, while tone is the way you communicate. For a highly technical yet imaginative, creative company such as technology developer Silicon Audio, the brand attributes are adventurous, daring, and intellectual, while the tone is conversational and confident when they describe how they work:

Silicon Audio: We create sensors that combine the best of century-old innovation with imaginative, modern engineering. At Silicon Audio, we live in a world of engineering, bound by the laws of physics but spared from the constraints of a specific industry. We begin by looking at current technology that's accepted and proven, but insufficient. And we ask: Why has it always been done this way? Can we make it better? How could something new cause a paradigm shift improvement?

This list of tone and voice examples can help you brainstorm and explore what defines your brand:

Example Brand Attributes:

- Adventurous
- Aggressive
- Classic
- Creative
- Customer-centered
- Didactic
- Fearless
- Honest

- Imaginative
- Intellectual
- Purposeful
- Precise
- Solutions-oriented
- Technical
- Traditional
- Trusted

Example Tones:

- Academic
- Approachable
- Clean

- Clear
- Conversational
- Confident

- Casual
- Descriptive
- Formal
- Friendly

- Inclusive
- Prestigious
- Professional

After establishing your brand attributes and tone, remind your team of them often. If you assign writers to produce content later, kick off content development with three to four slides that provide an overview of your personas, positioning, attributes, and tone so that your writers are aligned with the brand before they start writing. It's also helpful to show a few pieces of content that carry your attributes and tone as examples.

Remember that the tone you've chosen for your company may not be the natural tone that some of your engineers use, but you need to maintain a consistent voice in your marketing materials to deliver continuity for your customers. In the same way you maintain your company colors or a logo, keep your overall tone and language streamlined and familiar. To gain the trust of your customers, your content should sound like it's coming from the same company even if it's written by several different authors.

Best-in-class, brand-centric companies create style guides to document consistent language and product name use across all materials and bring in an editor who oversees all content for style and tone (see chapter 6 for more on editing).

Deliver on Your Brand Promise

Once you've established your brand attributes and tone, you can use these decisions to inform how you communicate.

Have you decided your brand will be "customer-centered" and "conversational?" Use a light tone and give best practices for specific customer needs. Also use the second-person point of view and include questions in your content. If your company introduces an exceptionally complex product, it will be you and your team's challenge to message that product in a conversational way, for example, to relate it to something customers already know or pose a jarring question that catches the interest of a prospect.

Have you decided your brand will be "solutions-oriented" and "academic"? Focus on technical "how-to" content to show your customers how they can approach or meet common challenges, such as this white paper from Wineman Technology: "Increase the Efficiency of Your Test Equipment with Test and Data Management Software."

Wineman Technology's solutions-oriented brand is supported by numerous how-to content pieces such as white papers and case studies.

If you're focusing on your proven history because you feel that your years of experience matter most to your prospects, you can strengthen your brand by showing customer success stories, solutions, and quotes each time you are tasked to market something the company has created. Give references for your work and showcase your awards and partnerships.

Develop Strong Messages That Convey a Powerful Brand

With your brand attributes, tone, and positioning defined, take some time to draft and finalize your differentiation pillars, elevator pitch, and segment messages.

1. Differentiation Pillars

Identify three differentiators that are key value propositions your company provides. These differentiators are what set you apart from competitors or in-house solutions. For each differentiator, create a headline and supporting details. Your company may have high-speed technology that gives customers a distinct advantage when using your products. Define "high speed" as a differentiator and decide how you will message it as a headline—you could make a comparison to existing technology or share a spec that gives buyers an idea of what speeds they can expect. Supporting bullets would document more specs, materials, and application examples that support your high speed.

Defining differentiators through this process will help your company communicate clearly and powerfully about the key benefits your company provides. Through the content development process, leverage the differentiator messaging.

2. Elevator Pitch

The elevator pitch is often the reason companies go through a complete branding exercise—they realize either they can't summarize what they do as a company, or they realize that everyone in the company shares a different story. The hardest part about creating a company pitch is keeping it short. But, by limiting the word count to thirty to sixty words, you create a pitch that's right and specific to your business.

The elevator pitch should:

- Make sense to strangers
- Be short
- Explain what your company does and what it's like to work with you
- Be memorable and inspire the prospect to visit your website to find out more
- Use the tone you identified for your brand

Say your pitch out loud.

Would you actually say these words? Is it quick enough? If not, adjust the pitch until you like how it sounds and it's sixty words or less (the closer to thirty words, the better).

Use this pitch consistently throughout your marketing materials. This message will become visible to your customers and allow them to start articulating your brand for you. They'll be able to tell peers what you do and why they should choose you.

Here are a few examples:

He3Labs: Navigate Blockchain. Transform your Industry. He3Labs brings the benefits of blockchain to real-world businesses with distributed ledger technology solutions for every industry. We assess, architect, and develop blockchain solutions that bring the power of enterprise-level security, auditability, and scale to any business.

Wineman Technology: Your product success is dependent on real-world performance. Evaluate your product's future performance today with test systems and fully simulated test environments from Wineman Technology to get a better product to market faster.

3. Segment Messages

With your brand positioning, differentiators, and elevator pitch defined and finalized, the next step is to create segment messaging. Segment messages take your corporate message and translate it to a specific product/product family, industry, application, partner, or any subset of your audience that has specific needs. Bring the owners of three to five segments into the branding committee and present to them the defined corporate position and messaging, and then discuss how that message should be tweaked to speak specifically to the nuances of their audience or product. Initial questions for this discussion include:

- What questions do you hear most often about this segment?
- What are customers' biggest pain points in this segment?
- How do you solve problems in this segment?
- How are your solutions/approach different?

Use the answers to create a headline message and sixty-word pitch for each segment. Here's an example from Hallam-ICS, where you can see the company's thirty-word elevator pitch and then a segment message for one of their service areas, Arc Flash Assessments. Hallam-ICS ultimately created five segment messages, one for each of their key service areas.

Elevator Pitch: Hallam-ICS is an engineering and automation company that designs MEP systems for facilities and plants, engineers control and automation solutions, and ensures safety and regulatory compliance through arc flash studies, commissioning, and validation.

Segment Message: *Certified Electrical Safety Experts*—At Hallam-ICS, we are passionate about electrical safety—the risks associated with complacency are too great to ignore. We perform detailed arc flash assessments and implement cost-effective solutions for short-term and long-term arc flash mitigation. We create and evaluate comprehensive computer models of existing systems and provide updated AutoCAD single lines for document control. Our certified electrical safety trainers help meet OSHA and NFPA 70E requirements and carry the burden of electrical safety in your facility so you can focus on your business output.

Storytelling: Creating a Narrative

Your brand should have a narrative or story that speaks to the problems your customers face, the solutions you provide, and the results your solutions drive.

It's easy to make your brand story all about you, but successful storytelling reframes your story to make your customers the heroes, instead of you or your product or service.

Think of your favorite movie. It probably loosely contains a character with some sort of physical, emotional, or mental problem (that's your customer). Your customer encounters a guide in the form of a person, idea, book, and so on (this is you). Through the story, the guide gives the customer a plan (that's your product or service), which the customer follows to succeed.

Your favorite movie or book starts its story with the customer, so compel your audience by starting your company story that way, too.

For example, I could tell you: *WirelessABC is a wireless connectivity company that creates top-of-the-line wireless connectivity solutions for consumer IoT devices. I could tell you that we have great technology and we work with big companies and that you can trust us, and that we value whatever you value. I could tell you that we care about bandwidth and we have good processes and we will give you a great product. And again, you really can trust us.*

That story was all about the company and what it does but not why that story should matter to a prospect. Instead, I could tell you: *The smart thermostat, outlet, watch, and fitness tracker you added to your household this year make your life easier and more entertaining, and you probably love them. You love experiencing them. Until they fail you.*

When a device fails to connect to the network, all the good it has ever done for you fades in seconds in light of the time and frustration it costs you to troubleshoot it.

At WirelessABC, we know that the reliability of your product's wireless connection is absolutely imperative to the success of your brand. We've developed best-in-class wireless connectivity solutions based on industry-standard technology to meet the most stringent standards and conditions. Our customers include Samsung, Apple, and Nike, all of which have grown their revenue 400 percent in two years on products that use our connectivity solutions.

The second version is more compelling. It touches on specific details that relate to customers' everyday concerns, and it's more impactful. To create a story about your company, you need to revisit your target customer personas, research specific pain points to amplify your customers' problems, make your customers the heroes, and position yourself as the guide.

1. Identify Your Target Customer

Review your personas and positioning statement to identify who your customers are and where they are in the buyer's journey. Determine whether they are decision makers or influencers, pinpoint their industries, and research their company sizes.

2. Amplify the Problem

Begin to think like your customers. What keeps them up at night? What happens if they don't solve their problems? What is happening in the industry to companies like them or products like theirs? Begin to articulate this problem. In the example above with WirelessABC, the prospect's challenge is to find a partner to provide wireless connectivity. If they don't choose the solution that accurately meets their needs, consumers may experience unreliable connectivity, the issues will worsen and result in failed products, and failed products will ultimately lead to a failed brand. The connectivity problem ends in sheer mayhem and tangible profit loss.

3. Make Your Customers the Heroes

Your customers want to succeed at their jobs. They want to do well, make their companies money, and be responsible for a really successful product. Articulate what this would look like for them. In our example, this is reliable connectivity from a reliable provider that eases their worries and provides a solution that's seamlessly integrated into the product for a no-fail user experience.

In your story, keep the thread focused on your specific customer—a person with a name—who's having a conversation with you. This helps you avoid lengthy lists and caveats with unnecessary detail.

4. Position Yourself as the Authority

You made the problem a big one, and your customers need help. Position yourself as their guide while they develop into heroes. Tell them what you offer and then give them some examples. Instead of saying you have rugged application capability, tell them your users have maintained connectivity in oil wells 5,000 feet deep into the ground. Give them specific visuals. Instead of telling them to trust you, tell them that companies like Ford or IBM trust your technology. These examples go a long way.

5. Remember That Storytelling Is Repetitive

Brands create loyalty from customers who talk about what they love. Your brand isn't about what you say; it's about what others say about you.

Strong brands created by smart marketers repeat their brand message over and over for years or decades. Your marketing gives your customers the language they need to talk about you and share their successes. Repeat customers who like to talk about their successes are fantastic marketing for your business, so give them a story they can share.

Silex Technology's homepage effectively showcases its brand based on the message, "When It Absolutely Must Connect," followed by the statement that with Silex, customers get devices that deliver a "completely connected, always-on experience." Throughout all its content, Silex highlights connection.

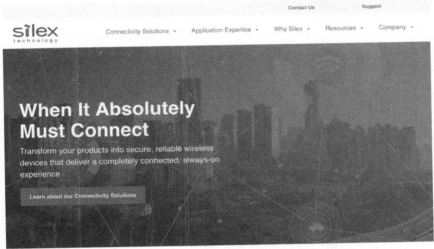

Silex Technology's homepage showcases their brand message.

Silex identified that its customers' greatest fear is to create a wireless device—be it a pacemaker, a fitness watch, or anything else—deliver it to an end user, and have the user experience downtime in network connectivity. A connection that isn't reliable would ruin its product and possibly its brand. So, Silex consistently relies on messaging about the "completely connected, always-on experience" offered by its embedded wireless and connectivity solutions.

Chances are, the internal Silex team will grow bored with this message in six months. Team members will begin having conversations about changing their message or launching a new campaign. But their audience, at this point, will barely have heard Silex's message. What if Intel abandoned "Intel Inside" after two quarters? It wouldn't be embedded in your mind as it is after a decade of marketing. Remind your team that these messages come from your brand position, which is foundational to your company, and they don't need to change often.

Now that you've defined your brand, you can begin to create content that supports your organization and draws in prospects.

Chapter 3
CREATE YOUR CONTENT MARKETING PLAN

Half or more of the buyer's journey happens before the prospect engages directly with a salesperson at a company, according to the research study *2020 Smart Marketing for Engineers: Critical Insight to Engage Engineers in a New Decade* published by IEEE Globalspec and TREW Marketing. During this time, buyers are consuming your content and forming opinions about your company and the solutions you offer. Once salespeople engage with prospects, they use even more content to win trust, preference, and ultimately new and repeat business.

Considering the importance of content to the buyer's journey, you'll want to devote time, attention, and strategic thought to your content plan. That may sound like an overwhelming task, but never fear! This chapter breaks down each step of the content planning process and provides framework tools to help inspire creativity and build consensus among your planning team members.

Content Planning Process

You can think of content planning as a microcosm of marketing planning. Some companies tackle both as one large process, while others work on their content plans downstream from their marketing planning. Either way is effective, but it is key to establish your marketing goals before developing your content plan. Both should be directly aligned to your business goals.

To develop your content plan, first establish a planning committee of three to five people from your organization. For smaller companies, this will likely be an executive, a marketing leader, and one to two other people who are closest to your audience persona, such as sales, product marketing, or service delivery. Gather this group in perhaps a half-day strategy session, roll up your sleeves, and start planning.

SWOT Analysis

Begin your planning process by identifying current content marketing strengths, weaknesses, opportunities, and threats (SWOT). This analysis helps you prioritize focus areas and determine key initiatives to strengthen your marketing program and content marketing plan.

When creating your content marketing SWOT, consider the following marketing areas:

- Content quantity and quality
- SEO (organic traffic, domain authority)
- Website traffic and engagement
- Lead generation and conversion
- Social presence and content promotion
- Database quality and engagement
- Partner marketing collaboration

In the example SWOT below, this company publishes a regular cadence of content promoted through channels such as enewsletters. The

MARKETING SWOT ANALYSIS

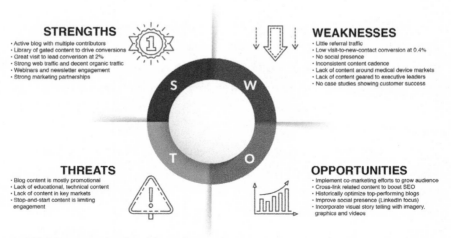

STRENGTHS
- Active blog with multiple contributors
- Library of gated content to drive conversions
- Great visit to lead converison at 2%
- Strong web traffic and decent organic traffic
- Webinars and newsletter engagement
- Strong marketing partnerships

WEAKNESSES
- Little referral traffic
- Low visit-to-new-contact conversion at 0.4%
- No social presence
- Inconsistent content cadence
- Lack of content around medical device markets
- Lack of content geared to executive leaders
- No case studies showing customer success

THREATS
- Blog content is mostly promotional
- Lack of educational, technical content
- Lack of content in key markets
- Stop-and-start content is limiting engagement

OPPORTUNITIES
- Implement co-marketing efforts to grow audience
- Cross-link related content to boost SEO
- Historically optimize top-performing blogs
- Improve social presence (LinkedIn focus)
- Incorporate visual story telling with imagery, graphics and videos

A SWOT analysis should evaluate the current state of your marketing program. This chart shows examples of statements for each section of the SWOT.

company's marketers have some issues with content coverage across key strategic business growth areas, and their content is not doing much to pull in and convert new contacts. One of their opportunities is to co-market with technology partners to address this gap. They may be detracting visitors through their promotion-oriented blog content.

If you're just getting started, you may not have many strengths, but spend time brainstorming opportunities with the contacts or partnerships you do have.

Set Objectives and KPIs

Once your SWOT analysis is complete, you are ready to establish content marketing objectives. Successful content plans contain objectives that tie directly to your marketing goals. What do you hope to achieve by developing your content?

Your objectives can be externally focused, internally focused, or perhaps a mix of both. Each of your objectives should have an associated KPI that you can easily measure over time. By identifying specific KPIs for your content objectives, you can gauge where to double down, troubleshoot, or divest in poor performing content pieces and tactics. Chapter 10 covers measuring these objectives in more detail.

Here is an example of content goal setting in action:

- **Marketing Goal #1**: Grow thought leadership in the medical components market
- **Content Objectives**: Create content on trends, regulations, and our reliable solutions
- **KPIs**: 30 percent conversion on gated medical content, double the number of medical contacts
- **Marketing Goal #2**: Increase lead generation on website by 20 percent

- **Content Objectives**: Create and promote one pillar page and two gated pieces of content
- **KPIs**: Increase the number of visits to pillar page, 20 percent conversion on gated content, lead grow

If you are not sure how to create marketing goals or content objectives to support your revenue goals, consider running a pipeline analysis of conversion rates between each stage in the buyer's journey. To do this, establish a time period, start with revenue, and work your way backward through the following calculations:

Calculate Leads to Revenue Converison Rate

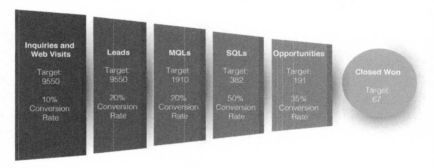

Goals:
New Customer Revenue: $5M
Avg. Sales Price: $75,000
Closed Won Contracts: 67

Working backward from your revenue will help you gain a realistic goal for healthy web traffic.

Topic Clusters: Framework for Content Brainstorming

When your objectives are in place, it is time to map out your content. We recommend using a topic cluster framework for numerous reasons. Similar in structure to a mind map, the topic cluster framework is an excellent tool for brainstorming with your team about content themes, topics, and subtopics because you can visually map their relationships.

Once implemented, a content plan developed through topic clusters ultimately helps your target personas easily find the information they need by carrying those content relationships through to your website. These connections help demonstrate your deep expertise to the web visitor, and the relational manner of the content connections improves your search engine rankings.

You will create several topic clusters as part of your content planning. The number depends on your marketing goals and how many marketing campaigns and personas you've developed. At a minimum, plan for one topic cluster per persona.

On a quest to deliver the most authentic results possible, search engine algorithms are routinely changing. In the recent past, we were all using a keyword-centric approach that involved researching keywords based on business solutions and traffic volume and then seeding those keywords throughout our content and web metadata. This keyword strategy performed well with Google for a decade, but changing search patterns inspired Google to alter its search algorithms.

People are searching differently than they did when the common practice was to target keywords only. With voice search (Hey, Siri! Hello, Alexa!), people are asking full questions or using specific, detailed phrases as opposed to a few keywords to find what they need. Smarter machine-learning algorithms that recognize location and aggregate past searches from a greater population to serve up similar topics and phrases are leading to the best search results.

To be found in this new age of relational search, you need to use topic clustering as the primary tool for your organic SEO strategy. This methodology focuses on identifying content themes that your customers care about and you're an expert in, creating deep content topics around these themes, and building relationships between those topics via cross-linking on your site.

This topic connectivity helps serve up content to your web visitors along the buyer's journey, provides context, and establishes your expertise in a particular area. It also alerts Google that there is a semantic relationship between your content pieces, which shows you are a trusted authority on a topic. When one page does well in search, the others are boosted, too. All ships rise in a trending topic cluster!

Now that you are up to speed with the many wonders of topic clustering, you need to create one. First, choose a core theme relevant to your audience persona in which you are an expert. This might be a solution you offer or an industry trend related to your solutions. Next, identify six to ten topics related to that theme. If you come up with too many (>fifteen), your theme is probably too broad, and you need to break things up into two topic clusters.

Topic Cluster Template

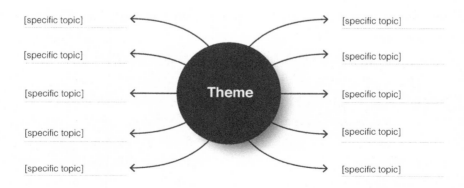

To create a topic cluster, start by mapping a central theme and related content topics.

In the example above, the core theme is "Managing Obsolescence," and the topics surrounding the theme, such as "The Cost of Not Upgrading Your System," are all potential content topics tied to that theme.

Map Content Along the Buyer's Journey: Framework for Content Form Factors

Next, you need to consider how the content topics in your topic cluster fall along the buyer's journey to ensure that you have coverage along all stages. Then you can identify the specific type of content you need to create for each topic (blog, white paper, video, etc.).

Identify key messages and content assets for each stage in the buyer's journey.

Let's dive into these stages in more detail:

1. Attract Visitors with Content

As buyers begin their journey in the discovery phase, they will likely find your website through a search engine. Once there, they will need to pinpoint a solution to a technical issue, research an industry trend, or explore a product or service you offer. Help the visitor quickly understand who you are and the solutions you offer and then show off your expertise. All this high-level content should be easy to find and access. Include a next-step call to action (CTA) to lead visitors into deeper content. Some of this content may be gated to entice the unknown visitor to become a known contact. Chapter 9 offers more information on CTAs.

Examples of early-stage content:

- Top- and mid-level web pages
- Blogs featuring how-to articles, tips and tricks, and best practices
- Case studies
- Short videos featuring product/solution demos
- Infographics featuring research or trends with supporting data
- Thought leadership trend pieces

2. Convert Leads with Content

As your buyers progress to the Evaluate stage, your company is now known to them. They will return to your site because they found useful information and are seeking more or because they are considering your product or service as a potential fit for their needs. Either way, you have earned their trust and attracted them back to your site. With this progression, you have an even better opportunity to convert these visitors into known prospects through gated content.

As the perceived value of a piece of content rises, so does the amount of personal information a web visitor is willing to share to access it. When deciding whether to gate content, you need to think about the level of technical effort the content took to create. Did this white paper require the involvement of subject-matter expert engineers? Is it more in-depth than your free content? Does it offer valuable how-to information or technical tips that your audience desires and can't easily find elsewhere? Chapter 8 offers the latest research on how engineers interact with forms and provides tips on how to improve your form completes.

Examples of mid-stage content:

- Technical white papers
- ebooks
- Tutorials
- Webinars
- Research reports and surveys
- Technical project-related templates (for example, reference designs, CAD drawings)
- Email nurturing

3. Close Prospects with Content

As prospects move into the late stage of their pre-purchase decisions, the conversation is passed from marketing channels (for example, website, emails) to a salesperson. As you'll discover in chapter 10, content still plays a critical role, but it's delivered in a one-to-one as opposed to a one-to-many manner. Some of the same content pieces previously mentioned are certainly used by sales as this point; however, you may identify new ideas for special pieces of content shared only during this phase.

Examples of late-stage content:

- Customer testimonials
- ROI studies
- Proposals
- In-depth, more specific case studies

4. Retain and Delight Customers with Content

Your content plan doesn't stop after you've closed a new client. Nurture your client relationships and create advocates for your company by sending relevant, helpful content. Given the nudge, customers will dig deeper into your site to discover what else you offer that helps them do their jobs better, faster, or cheaper, and this may lead to them purchasing more products and services or becoming promoters.

Ideas for client-nurturing content include:

- Getting started tips and tricks
- Online training or course material
- Industry trends
- New products or services
- Company news
- Survey requesting their feedback

Research Data on
Content Types

Research shows that engineers enjoy a variety of content types. In the study below, engineers were asked to weigh in on the value of different types of content when conducting research for their jobs. The "very" and "somewhat valuable" answers in the figure below show

Most engineers like to view content in the formats that best suit the material.

that engineers find most of the content types valuable. Notice that there were very few content types ranked as "not valuable"—engineers really do like their content! Though there is some variance by age, with Millennial engineers showing higher preference for video content, most engineers like to view content in the formats that best suit the material.

Content Title/Type	Content Type	Stage	Persona	Call-to-Action
OEE and Downtime Tracking	Blog	Attract	Plant Manager Micheal	ROI of MES White Paper
Security for IoT and ICS	Blog	Attract	Process Control Chrisl	Cybersecurity White Paper
The Role of AI in the Modern Factory	Blog	Attract	Plant Manager Micheal	Smart Factory Fireside Chat
System Migration With Minimal Downtime	Case Study	Attract	Process Control Chris	Migration Demo Video
Turning Plant Data into Business Insights	White Paper	Convert	Plant Manager Micheal	ROI of MES White Paper
7 Point Checklist for SCADA Security	Video	Convert	Process Control Chris	Onsite Consultation
SCADA Solution Demo Video	Gated Piece	Convert	Process Control Chris	Spec Sheet

Example of content topics mapped to content type, buyer's journey stage, and persona.

Now that you've thought about which content formats are the most effective for your topics based on where they fall along the buyer's journey, you need to label each topic in your cluster with the type of content you'll use.

Topic Cluster Example

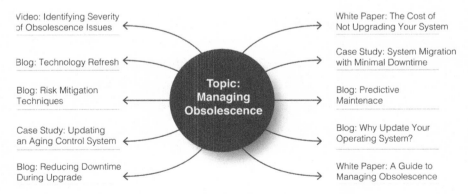

Once you've identified your content theme and subtopics, add a content type (video, blog, etc.) by each topic on your topic cluster.

Build a Content Calendar

Once you complete your topic clusters, the final content planning step is to build a content calendar. You will rely on this tool greatly to manage content implementation details such as ownership and deadlines. Beyond its project management uses, a content calendar serves as a quick reference to the strategy behind each content piece. Include the related theme, persona, stage of buyer's journey, and CTA in your calendar, such as the example calendar below.

Example Content Calendar

Content Type	Topic	Writer	SME	Campaign	Persona	Stage	Due Date	Publish Date
Blog Post	When Reliability Counts (Applications)	Jen	Phillip	Maintenance	Oil/Gas Engineer Ethan	Discover	1-Oct	8-Oct
Blog Post	Hidden Costs Of Fluid Handling	Jen	James	ROI Of Outsourcing	VP Victor	Discover	8-Oct	15-Oct
Blog Post	Cost/Efficiency Gains Of Custom Fluid Handling Solutions	Jen	James	ROI Of Outsourcing	Oil/Gas Engineer Ethan	Discover	22-Oct	29-Oct
Blog Post	Blog Promoting White Paper	Mark	James	Sustainability	VP Victor	Evaluate	29-Oct	5-Nov
White Paper	Environmental Considerations For New Oil And Gas Machinery	Mark	James	Sustainability	VP Victor	Evaluate	29-Oct	5-Nov
Case Study	Underwater Drilling Long-Term Maintenance Application	Mark	Phillip	Maintenance	Oil/Gas Engineer Ethan	Decide	5-Nov	12-Nov
Pillar Page	Trends In Oil And Gas Engineering	Sarah	Rick	Sustainability	Oil/Gas Engineer Ethan	Evaluate	12-Nov	19-Nov

Use a content calendar for project management and a content strategy quick reference guide.

Every piece of content should have a CTA, which directs readers to take an action you specify after consuming the initial content. Calling out the CTA in your plan helps keep this important step top of mind and shows how the specific content pieces connect. Use whatever tool is most comfortable, whether that be project management software such as Trello or a simple Excel spreadsheet.

Content Planning Pro Tips

- **Review Personas**: Look back at your persona definitions and review their goals, pain points, and needs again. Be sure you addressed their concerns with your content topics.

- **Ask Sales**: Pull in some of your experienced salespeople. They are closest to your target personas and have valuable input regarding which topics and types of content resonate well in each stage of the cycle.

- **Vary Free and Gated Content**: Include a good mixture of free and gated content, so that you not only engage your audience as a whole but also convert prospects to leads.

- **Vary Content Types**: Your content types should vary because not all engineers interact with content the same way. Some prefer detailed, long-form content; some like videos or visual content; and some lean toward short, scannable content with drill-down links.

Replacing the Sales Funnel with the Sales Flywheel

Reprinted by permission of Harvard Business Review.
From "Replacing the Sales Funnel with the Sales Flywheel" by Brian Halligan, November 2018
Copyright ©2018 by Harvard Business Publishing; all rights reserved.

I've been using the sales funnel for 28 years, my whole career. This year, I retired the funnel—threw it a party, gave it a gold watch, and congratulated it on its move to a condo in Florida.

It was the right thing to do.

For one thing, in an era when trust in traditional sources has eroded in government, media, and in companies and the marketing they employ word-of-mouth from trusted peers wields greater clout than ever.

For another, the funnel fails to capture momentum. A boss of mine used to say, "The sun rises and sets on the quarter." By the end of a quarter, she had wrung every ounce of energy out of marketing, and we started the next quarter from a standstill with no momentum and no leverage.

That's no longer true. After years of inbound marketing, your company has assets: evergreen content; backlinks to your site; social media followings; and, of course, customers who advocate for your brand. For many of us, our marketing departments could take a vacation for a month, and new visitors and leads would continue to come in, and existing customers would continue to refer new business. That's momentum.

The Flywheel

These days, instead of talking about the funnel, we talk about the flywheel. For us, flywheel is a powerful metaphor. The flywheel was used by James Watt over 200 years ago in his steam engine, the invention that powered the Industrial Revolution. It is highly efficient at capturing, storing, and releasing energy.

Using a flywheel to describe our business allows me to focus on how we capture, store, and release our own energy, as measured in traffic and leads, free sign-ups, new customers, and the enthusiasm of existing customers. It's got a sense of leverage and momentum. The metaphor also accounts for loss of energy, where lost users and customers work against our momentum and slow our growth.

I've become obsessed with two dynamics that make our flywheel spin fast: force and friction.

Force

The more force you apply to a flywheel, the more places on it where you add force, the faster it spins.

When I started my career, the most profitable application of force was in sales. Back in the 1990s, sales reps had a lot of information, while customers had relatively little. Sales reps leveraged that information gap to create a lot of trust. It made a ton of sense to hire a lot of reps back then.

Around 2005, marketing became a bigger force driving growth. In many industries, the sales rep and the customer now had more or less the same information at the same time. Competitive advantage went to those marketers who created useful content to pull prospects in.

Today, it's shifting again. Now, delighted customers are the biggest new driver of growth.

I'm a sales and marketing guy, so it makes sense that HubSpot's early priorities reflected my instincts, with all our energy and force applied to sales and marketing, trying to close as many customers as possible. These days, we've shifted our center of gravity away from that and applied more force towards delighting our existing customers, knowing that's the best way to find new customers.

I made a couple mistakes along the way. First, I just said, "hey, we're going to be a 'delight' company!" The intention was right, but there was no operational impact.

Second, I assigned this to our customer service department. I said, "you've to fix this problem, we've got to delight our customers." Neither of those things worked.

What worked was getting the whole organization behind it—especially Sales and Marketing.

Take our commission plan, for example. In 2015, a sales rep earned commission on everything they closed. Now, we've made two important tweaks to it: a carrot and a stick. The stick was very unpopular. If a sales rep closed an account, and that account cancelled within eight months, the company would "claw back" that commission. Painful, but effective.

The carrot was easier, and also effective. The sales reps who do the best job at setting expectations, who have high retention rates and the happiest customers, receive a kicker, they got paid at a higher rate.

That carrot and stick have changed how we think about the "force" part of our flywheel. Our sales reps are focused not only on closing customers, but on delighting customers.

We've done something similar with the quality of our leads. Prospects that are more likely to be successful customers get a higher lead score, rather than leads that are simply likely to close. We measure the success of our marketing based upon the volume of those most-likely-to-succeed leads.

Friction

The second thing James Watt would recommend is to eliminate friction in your flywheel.

I'm a true believer in low friction. I woke up this morning on my Purple mattress. I put on my Warby Parker eyeglasses, picked up my phone and played Spotify. I made my way to my bathroom and shaved with my Dollar Shave Club razor. I reached into my closet and put on my new outfit from Trunk Club, and then I got in a Lyft and came to work.

These six companies have woven their way into my daily life. They are all fewer than 10 years old; they all sell relatively undifferentiated commodities; and they are all growing like a weed? How do they do it? What's the secret handshake?

It's friction—they've taken all the friction out of their flywheel. When I bought that Purple mattress, there was almost zero friction in the process. I did it in a few minutes online; they shipped it to my home; and if I decided to return it, the process promised to be simple and hassle-free.

Two years ago, I bought my previous mattress from a traditional seller—a so-called full-service store. But full service means handoffs between humans, it means haggling. Buyers have become much less patient, and less forgiving of friction.

All of these examples are B2C. If your business is B2C, the train is about to leave the station. You've got to get 90% of the friction out of your model. If you're B2B, the train is parked in the station, but it's leaving soon.

One of my favorite business school professors used to say, "If you want to build a great company, your product has got to be ten times better than the competition." Today, that advice feels out of date. If you want to build a great company in 2018, your customer experience has to be ten times lighter than the competition. It used to be what you sell that really matters, now it's how you sell that really matters.

Section Two

Create Sticky Content

Chapter 4
PREPARE TO WRITE

Once you've identified your personas, defined your brand, and created a content plan, it is time to get writing. To write effectively (and efficiently, as managing this content development probably isn't the sole focus of your job!), you need to understand who should write your content, the fundamentals of strong content, the nuances of specific types of content, and all the ins and outs of editing and refining your content.

You likely have many SMEs and levels of marketing expertise floating around your organization. For that reason, content often becomes everyone's problem (read: no one's problem). There are a lot of hallway conversations and a lot of big ideas but very few actual words on paper. Designating who creates your content and how it gets created ensures that those big ideas come to fruition with words on a page.

Options for Content Creators

Think outside the box. Each of the many options for marketing content development offers both benefits and weaknesses:

1. SMEs create all content
2. Marketing creates all content
3. Marketing completely outsources content
4. Marketing leads content creation with support and expertise from SMEs
5. Marketing and SMEs create content hand-in-hand with outsourced partner

The first three options provide Lone Ranger situations with little accountability or support. Don't do them. Having SMEs (untrained in marketing) create every piece of content is laborious and expensive. They're so entrenched in the details of their products or services that it's difficult for them to take a step back and produce content that's engaging to prospects. And their time is highly valuable, their billable rates are high, and they shouldn't spend hours working through specific sentences and the flow of a concept.

At the other extreme, when marketing creates all content (or blindly outsources all content) without input from SMEs, it's nearly impossible to get the deep, specific product or technical detail needed for meaningful content. For example, in the case of marketing to engineers, marketers often digest the specifications or benefits of a new product and generate a news release headline with a superlative: "New signal generator creates the fastest high-speed serial data signal." Most engineers would rework this headline. Even if their signal generator *is* the fastest on the market today, they know that their target audience (also engineers) will balk at a claim of fastest, highest, or best. They know that technically there *may* be a faster (albeit less efficient) solution found by combining different filters and instruments, and they don't want to be technically incorrect. These nuances are lost when marketing or an outsourced firm creates all content without the input of the SMEs. Remember, your contacts can spot "marketing speak" with the trained eye of a gazelle watching for predators at the water hole. Often, it just takes one whiff of marketing speak to send them running to the hills. Ultimately, the content produced from these Lone Ranger efforts is typically inaccurate or fluffy, immediately eroding trust in your brand.

The last two options allow for a partnership between marketing and SMEs, ultimately using the best skills of both. Whether you choose to outsource your marketing is a function of resources and requirements. If your content marketing goals and plans are significant, you will need either a well-trained internal team or an outsourced partner.

Gain Marketing Buy-In from SMEs

To create high-quality, trustworthy, and accurate content that technical buyers value, you need to involve SMEs. After years of asking the question, our research consistently shows that engineers around the world trust content written by engineering experts at vendor companies more than any other types of content.

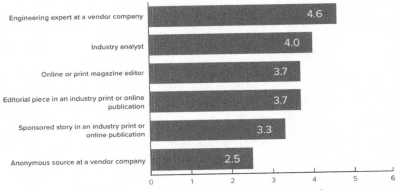

Rank your level of trust in content that is written or published by the following, where a rank of 6 is your highest level of trust, and a rank of 1 is your lowest.

Engineers trust content created by other engineers over other content.

However, we hear repeatedly from marketers at technical companies that their number one content marketing challenge is finding an SME with time to research and write content. To overcome this challenge and achieve the marketing buy-in needed from SMEs so they'll participate in content development, the best courses of action are:

1. Make a Match

Pair your SME with a marketing writer who can do the heavy lifting on writing. Through interviews and reviews, the writer can learn the important information and data from the SME to produce a high-quality technical piece of content that the engineer likes while minimizing the actual time the SME is required to spend on the project.

2. Ask for Source Material

Prepare for further conversations with your SMEs by asking them for source material. They may have given presentations on the topic you're covering, created datasheets, or curated supplemental material for other aspects of their jobs that you can use to understand the topic and ask the best questions possible later in the process.

3. Work with Your SMEs the Way They Work Best

Be as sensitive as you can to your SMEs' communication preferences. A startup CEO who has garnered funding from multiple rounds of VC pitching is probably great at talking. Don't ask the CEO to complete an interview questionnaire; instead, send over questions beforehand and ask to have a conversation, whether that's an in-person meeting or a phone call during the CEO's commute home. Record the call so you can keep the conversation moving and natural. In contrast, R&D engineers want every fact to be 100 percent accurate and complete. They'll often decline to answer a question if they don't know the exact answer. Email them a few questions and ask them to respond in writing or set up a time to discuss the questions in person. Often, they'll answer your questions precisely if given the opportunity to do so in writing.

4. Show Results

Using basic marketing metrics, you can recognize and reward the time your SMEs invested by showing the impact of their efforts on the business. This can be as simple as sharing traffic and leads data. If you have more sophisticated pipeline measurements in place, you can even track original content conversion all the way to revenue. We'll cover more on content measurement in chapter 10. By using ROI metrics on traffic and leads to demonstrate the impact of content on the business and revenue, you can make a strong argument based on dollars to convince your leadership team that increasing SME time allocated for content marketing is a smart move!

Guiding Principles for Sticky Content

Technical content that appeals to your audience and gives your prospects the information they need must be carefully planned.

Statistically, technical buyers consume up to sixteen sales assets before making a final purchase decision. For most engineers, over half of the buying process happens online before they speak to a company. Your prospects must be able to engage with the content you create. Through this content, you can compel them with your thought leadership, inform them with your technical depth, and build confidence in them with your experience. For your content to stick, it should meet a need, tell a story, and educate the customer.

Great content has the following characteristics:

- **Relevant**: Your content should fill a need for your prospects. Think back to your personas, their challenges, and what you can do for them; these factors should form the basis for your content topics. Instead of sharing the same view on a topic your competitors already covered, build on what's already out there.

- **Compelling**: Your content should drive action. Write content that offers helpful insight and leads to next steps. Combine facts and details with specific use cases to illustrate your point and add credibility. As much as possible, connect emotionally with your audience to make your content easy to consume.

- **Findable**: Engineers search for answers to specific problems, so research and choose long-tail keywords (three- and four-word phrases that are hyper-specific to your audience and what you sell) that filter out the more general audiences for your content. Include one to three keywords in your content (especially in the headline, intro paragraph, subheads, and meta descriptions) to help prospects searching for information find your content.

- **Consistently Published/Updated**: Content gains traction when you publish consistently over time. Create content according to your content plan and consistently link to other related content on your site.

- **Branded**: Your content should follow the tone and voice you set out to convey in your branding exercise. Your brand message and values should come through in each piece of content you create, which will help readers begin to associate with your company and what you provide.

> Follow the 90 percent educational and 10 percent promotional rule to grow thought leadership and build trust.

- **Educational**: Follow the 90 percent educational and 10 percent promotional rule to grow thought leadership and build trust. While writing, always ask the question, "So what?" Make sure you're sharing how the topic affects your prospects' main concerns, whether those are quality, cost, schedule, or reputation.

- **Readily Available Throughout Their Journeys**: Think about the range of content your prospects need throughout the buying cycle—from understanding their challenges to evaluating vendors, partners, or suppliers to physically programming or connecting a solution—and develop content for each phase.

- **Readable**: We're all pressed for time. Readers take just a few seconds to determine whether content will be valuable to them, so write in a style that's easy to scan.

Before writing each piece of content, define its intention. Evaluate your personas and which types of content you need to guide them through the buyer's journey.

Identify the content you need to create, define your key messages for the piece, pinpoint the audience based on your personas, set the tone, create an expectation for length, and develop a timeline. These decisions help you both define and guide your content development before you even begin writing.

Chapter 5
LEARN TO WRITE BY CONTENT TYPE

During the content planning process, you identified types of content and specific topics that are relevant to your audiences. This chapter examines the nuances of creating specific types of content.

For each content type, explore the following elements:

- Name and description of the content type
- Details at a glance:
- Buyer's journey stage (refer to the stages discussed in chapter 3: Discover, Evaluate, Decide, Advocate)
- Length
- Cost to reader
- Life span
- Time to create
- Common topics
- Best practices
- Final checklist

Use this chapter both as an overview and a reference that you can return to when you're writing or assigning writers to content.

Blog Posts

Blogging is the most effective way to increase your rank and search volume and establish your company as an expert in your industry. Because of these two purposes, blogging is both an art (topic selection and writing) and a science (publishing and promoting, covered in the next chapter). Your blog can convey several types of information including technical how-tos and best practices, industry viewpoints, product/solution updates, and company news.

What Is a Blog Post?

Blog posts are short pieces of content published on your site that give more information about topics of interest to your clients. Blogs can educate with technical posts, promote new content assets such as white papers and webinars by providing lighter education content that drives the visitor to a landing page, and communicate company news such as new products and events. Blog posts should heavily emphasize education, and promotional posts should be carefully laced with education components. An example of this would be to provide an event wrap-up that cites industry trends along with your own company's news.

- **Buyer's Journey Stage**: Discover (industry trends, best practices, tips and tricks); Evaluate (thought leadership, how-to)
- **Length**: 400 to 750 words; if you find yourself running way over, consider breaking up your material into a series or converting the piece into a white paper or other long-form piece
- **Cost to Reader**: Free
- **Life Span**: Two to three years
- **Time to Create**: One to two weeks

Blog Post Topics

- Lists of top themes or common problems
- Your take on industry events or topics
- Discussion of current trends or future possibilities
- Guides for doing something better
- Controversial topics or alternative opinions
- Thoughts exposing misconceptions about industries, solutions, or common practices
- Lessons learned or common mistakes

- Technical detail where your company excels (Note that technical blog posts will likely take more time and more involvement from your SME.)

Best Practices

Here are a few key considerations when creating this content:

1. Streamline the Information-Gathering Process

Ask your SME a few simple questions to get the information you want to include in a blog post. Within about thirty minutes, you should have the answers you need to put together your post draft. Ask for specific details to make your post more compelling: specs, thoughts on industry trends, or steps readers can follow. These all make your content more engaging for a reader.

When you're interviewing, never ask for information you could have found on your own. If the information is on Google, you should know it going *into* the interview or find it afterward. Also, be willing to employ the awkward pause during the interview. It's natural to avoid awkward silence, but if you allow silence to linger, you're likely to get details about something you weren't even aware you needed to know about your subject.

2. Be Interesting and Use Catchy Headlines

It seems like a no-brainer, but it's important to write about topics that interest your potential customers. Think outside the box. For example, while your customers may be manufacturing test and measurement equipment, they're also hiring experts to use that equipment, so consider writing a blog post about hiring the best engineer for the types of applications your customers are creating.

3. Give Your Take on Relevant Topics

If there's a news topic that's already popular in your industry, write a blog post about it so that when readers are searching for the topic, they come across your site. For example, if a prominent engineering school was granted $10 million for its robotics program and your company makes robotic medical devices, talk about how you think that university could spend its grant to further medical advancements. Or, if you're a software integrator and one of the platforms you integrate has a new release, write a post talking about how customers can use the features in that new version to better their businesses. This tactic is called news-jacking: capitalizing on the popularity of a topic to boost your sales and marketing success. Be sure to use the news topic in your headline for the best search results.

4. Be One of the First to Talk About a New Trend

Is there a new idea in the marketplace? A new product? A process once used in another space that could be applied to your industry? Share your thoughts and best practices on the topic first with a blog post.

5. Answer Questions Your Sales or Product Teams Constantly Get

If your teams find they're constantly answering certain questions or educating prospects about certain misconceptions, write a blog post about the topic. You'll gain not only a blog post but also a streamlined answer that sales can use or, better yet, that potential customers can find—along with your company—when they search for the topic.

6. Make It Readable

Use lists, bullet points, and short paragraphs to make your content scannable and readable.

7. Use Images and Graphics in Your Posts

You can't deny it: We humans love pictures. Pictures power social media. Visual content is revolutionizing social media and the ways that web content is consumed. When B2B and B2C marketers were asked how important visual content was to their content marketing strategies, 90 percent said visual content was either very important or absolutely necessary. Visual social networking sites such as Instagram and Pin-terest are so popular because people like pretty pictures and so does Google. Therefore, to grow the reach and shares of your posts, use com-pelling images that showcase the points you're making.

8. Repurpose Existing Content

If you've already created a white paper or a case study, summarize some of the points into a blog post. Or, tackle what a specific white paper topic means for a certain industry. This greatly minimizes the time you need from an SME resource.

9. Invite Others to Share Their Experience or Expertise as a Guest Blogger

As you work with customers and partners, consider inviting them to write a guest post on your blog. This practice builds community and provides a win-win for readers, you, and your client.

10. Reference Other Blog Posts—Both Yours and Others

Web content, particularly blog content, is meant to be dynamic. You enable visitors to "surf the web" when referencing your own and others' material in context. At the time you introduce a topic that likely needs further explanation, it's a good idea to hyperlink that content to either a page on your site that gives more detail or a credible third-party site. When you link to pages on your site or another's, it helps build your online recognition by earning links and increasing your web traffic and rank.

11. Include a Call to Action

Based on the nature of the content, this might be for a gated piece of con-tent, demo, or request to meet with an applications engineer. Use buttons or images for these CTAs to improve visibility and conversion rates.

Final Checklist

- Write an intriguing or catchy headline
- Keep your word count to around 400 to 600 words
- Include lists, subheads, and short paragraphs
- Include links to other blog posts, examples, or third-party content
- Include relevant images

Linear Actuators: Electric vs. Hydraulic

A quick Google search of this post's title will result in plenty of information to digest and a wide range of comparisons (and opinions) based on who is providing them. Obviously, suppliers have a bias toward what they sell, and users based on what they know best from past experience. Someone in agricultural equipment may choose hydraulic linear actuators exclusively, and someone in robotics only electric ball-screws.

Wineman Technology's blog homepage uses headlines and the first few sentences to grab the reader, leading them into the full post.

Infographics

As the world grows more digitized, we as marketers must fight harder for attention from our key audiences. This is not an easy task. Infographics pack a lot of information in an easy-to-scan visual format. Data also shows that infographics are an important piece in any content marketing strategy. Infographics are liked and shared three times more than other content types.

What Is an Infographic?

An infographic is a visual represen-
tation of data. Shared infographics
turn data and complicated subjects
into visually interesting content that
draws a reader's attention. Technical
content is easier to understand when
you present it visually to your audience. An infographic should break
down complicated data into simple
and concise points with pictures and
graphics that support that content.
Infographics can come in all sizes
and shapes, with varying levels of
detail. Before investing in an infographic, think back to your personas
and what type of information they
need (ROI versus technical detail versus industry information).

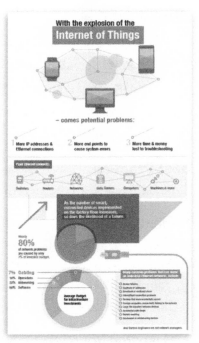

*This infographic shares multiple
data points and conclusions in
a graphic format..*

- **Buyer's Journey Stage**: Dis-
  cover (show the complexity of a problem, explore options for
  a solution, understand what goes into getting the solution you
  need)
- **Cost to Reader**: Infographics are considered free content and
  should not be gated behind a lead form
- **Life Span**: Because they are often data-rich and need to be
  updated heavily over time, infographics are usually relevant for
  twelve to eighteen months
- **Time to Create**: Four to six weeks

Infographic Topics

- Show a process
- Highlight small details of a large project
- Break down a large problem into smaller ones
- Show data about a specific topic
- Highlight trends

Best Practices

Here are a few key considerations when creating this content:

1. Identify a Topic

To create an infographic, you need to find a good topic that is core to your business and can be visually represented. Pinpoint the pages on your website that attract the most views and interactions and then brainstorm infographics that could make these pages even better.

2. Research Your Topic

Once you've determined your topic, do your research. Find facts and statistics that you want to include. This also helps you become a valuable resource on your topic. After you complete your research, sketch out your idea for an infographic on paper before starting the design process.

3. Hire a Designer

Infographics can be tedious and detailed. Even if you're handling the content yourself, consider contracting a designer to pull together the final image. Gather a few styles of infographics you like to provide ideas and direction.

Final Checklist

- Headline
- Cited data
- Icons and images
- Branded layout

Case Studies

You can have the world's greatest product, but if you can't show how customers are using and benefiting from it, you don't have much ground to stand on. Rarely do potential customers—especially engineers and scientists—want to be the first to use a new product, and journalists will tell you to call back when you have a customer example they can share with their readers.

What Is a Case Study?

Case studies are a great way to demonstrate how valuable your products or services are in the marketplace. They go beyond simple testimonials by showing real-life examples of how you were able to solve customers' problems and help them achieve success. With case studies, you highlight your successes in a way that can help an ideal potential customer move one step closer to becoming a new customer. Case studies range from 800 to 1,200 words and include images and customer attribution.

- **Length**: 800 to 1,200 words
- **Buyer's Journey Stage**: Discover (new solutions); Evaluate (potential solutions and ROI); Advocate (promote customer success)
- **Cost to Reader**: Case studies are considered free content and therefore should not require a form submit to view them
- **Life Span**: Depending on your industry, a well-written case study can have up to a five-year life span
- **Time to Create**: Two to three weeks plus the customer approval process

Case Study Topics

- Cost savings or time savings using your solutions
- Achieving new results with your solutions
- Specific industry applications

Best Practices

Here are a few key considerations when creating this content:

1. Be Choosy When Possible

When you are selecting a case study to write, choose a customer who will tell your story well. Find a customer who has significant, quantifiable results in an application that is relevant to the most people who can show other potential customers the value of your product or service. A well-known brand doesn't hurt.

2. Get Ready for the Ask

Communicate the marketing need for case studies to your sales team. As they're helping customers solve their applications with your products or services, mention how great it would be to highlight their finished projects as case studies. A salesperson may even ask to include a case study in a sales contract. This is especially helpful in the negotiation phase: When your customer is asking for a discount or "freebies" to throw in, you can ask in exchange to do a case study that benefits your company.

Also, communicate the mutual benefit of a case study for you and your customers. Case studies highlight the benefits of your products or services, but they also help customers showcase their successes. By posting the completed case studies on your website, you help improve your customers' web presence and further their company names.

Note that large companies, organizations with government or defense contracts, or customers that consider the use of your product part of their differentiators or trade secrets likely will not approve a case study for public publishing. Learn about the permissions and review process before you start writing. Another option is to write an anonymous case study and generally reference the company or organization without naming it specifically. While an anonymous case study is not as impactful as its branded counterpart, it is a good option to demonstrate your real-world experience and expertise.

3. Do the Work

Don't expect a customer to write a case study for you. If you want a case study that showcases the benefits of your products or services, you'll need to write it yourself. With this approach, you can easily include key messages that you've defined for your company.

Create an outline of your case study and then interview your customer to fill in any gaps. Make sure you can articulate:

- The problems your customer was trying to solve
- Other solutions they considered before choosing to partner with your company
- The new functionality or solution they now have because of your product
- The results they've achieved

4. Get to the Specifics

Write your case study in a way that potential customers can relate to and show a quantifiable result. Draw readers in with results-focused headlines highlighting cost or time savings, new achievements, or significant industry headaches that were averted, such as downtime, product loss, or measurement error.

5. Make Approval Easy

After you draft your case study, you'll need your customer to review it. When sending it for review, highlight specific areas for them to assess and include all images or screenshots you want to use. This way, you can get all the content reviewed and approved at once.

In addition, draft a specific quote that they can review and approve so that you can use that quote and its attribution on your website, in a flyer, or in a news release in the future.

Final Checklist

- Results-oriented headline
- Clear, one-sentence challenge
- Clear, one-sentence solution
- Up to 1,600 words explaining how your products or services solved the challenge
- Specific results include data as proof points (i.e., money savings, decreased time to market)
- Illustrations, images, charts or graphs with captions

A complete, designed case study with images.

Videos

Video content continues to grow in popularity, both in mainstream culture and with technical buyers. Why is this? The audio/visual nature of video is engrossing and lends itself well to communicating detailed or complex information. Additionally, Google's acquisition of YouTube, following an algorithm change to make video searchable makes this content easier than ever to find and consume. Google and YouTube occupy the number one and two spots for search engine popularity, respectively.

Video creation can be an intimidating undertaking to a small business, but it doesn't need to be so unapproachable. The slick, professionally produced videos of the 90s have given way to a diverse set of production outputs where content, not production quality, reigns supreme. That being said, there are clear best practices to ensure that your video provides a positive brand experience for the viewer.

What Is a Video?

Videos combine visual and audio content together to produce a memorable educational experience, and are often published on platforms like YouTube and company websites. They can include customer interviews, show how to use a product, or present a company overview or solution to a problem.

- **Length**: One and a half to twenty minutes
- **Buyer's Journey Stage**: Explore (corporate videos, testimonials/case studies, concept overviews, live video); Evaluate (product or solution demo, how-to); Advocate (training)
- **Cost to Reader**: Videos are typically considered free content and therefore should not have a lead form required to view them
- **Life Span**: Depending on the content, up to one to two years
- **Time to Create**: Six to eight weeks

Video Topics

- Evaluating solutions
- Product demo
- Company overview
- Executive profile
- Case study or customer profile

Best Practices

Here are a few key considerations when creating video content:

1. Match Your Video Goals with A Suitable Level of Production

Not every video requires high-end equipment or a production specialist, but some do. If your video is intended to demonstrate a product or show off your staff's technical expertise, your production effort may be on the low end. Conversely, if you are looking to create a corporate branding video for investors, more time and investment will be required to create the perfect piece. Here are some production approaches to consider:

Low Effort

- Employee delivering a short script
- Event presentation or expo floor interviews
- Recorded demo or presentation with voiceover narration

Medium Effort

- Animated video
- Static imagery and words set to music and voiceover

High Effort

- Onsite video capturing multi-faceted scenes, interviews
- Professional talent engaged for a formal, scripted production

2. Scripts and Storyboards Are Video's Best Friend

If your video is of the "talking head" variety, start with a written script rehearsed by the speaker. Consider that this script may be pulled from existing content such as a blog post which can be repurposed into a video.

If you video includes demos or other visuals, you'll need to map out where those visuals fall along with the script. Often this is done through storyboarding, where scenes are sketched (or mapped out) along with script development prior to production. At a regular pace, speakers cover about 150 words per minute—use this data point to map your script to the timing of your video.

3. Match Length with the Content Type

The rule of thumb for marketing videos has been to keep the length at two minutes or less. A 2016 study by Wistia showed a significant drop-off in viewership between two and three minutes. Vidyard reported that in 2018 the average length of videos published was four minutes, which was one-third shorter than in 2017. All this being said, the highest-performing videos on YouTube, across 1.3 million videos studied, averaged a whopping fourteen minutes long, according to a 2017 study by Backlinko.

So, what makes sense for your content? The best rule of thumb is to make your video just long enough to cover all the information, not any longer. For technically oriented videos, viewers are willing to stick around a bit longer (ten to twenty minutes), but with each minute that ticks by, you risk losing viewership. Consider sticking to the two or three most important points or create a series of related videos to avoid overwhelming your viewers.

4. Focus on Your Persona

For a demo video, start with the audience issue and work back to your solution. Begin with a common customer problem and show how your product solves it. Connect the product features to your viewers' lives and problems and show how your products fit into their lives.

Your script should incorporate a tone that best connects with your persona. For instance, this tone may be formal and structured or conversational. The set of your video, attire of your spokesperson, and other visual factors should also align with what would best resonate with your persona.

5. Quality

Regardless of the production effort you've selected for your video, there are minimum standards to meet regarding sound and picture quality. Make sure that the viewer can easily hear and see what is happening in your video. If your plan is to create low-cost videos with your smartphone, consider investing in plug-in microphones and lenses to boost the quality while keeping costs low. See the sidebar for more details on equipment.

6. Transcriptions and Captions—Key Parts of the Video Production Process

Transcripts of your video are key to serving the hearing impaired and helping search engines crawl your content more easily. You may be tempted to use the YouTube auto-transcribe service, but by this book's publish date is was abysmal at delivering accurate transcriptions. There are many low-cost software options out there such as Rev and Trint to consider.

Once you have your transcription completed it is time to tackle captioning. According to a study by Verizon Media and Publicis Media, 68 percent of people watch videos with the sound off when in a public place, and 25 percent of people watch videos with the sound off in a private space. Overall, they found that 80 percent of people are more likely to watch a video if captions are available. Take the time to use your video transcript to create complete subtitles, overlaid on the videos.

7. Use Native Videos Across Sites

Instead of publishing your video on YouTube and linking to it from other platforms like LinkedIn and Facebook, upload your video directly to your profile on those third-party sites. Uploading videos directly to each site creates a video gallery on the site and statistically increases engagement with the video, according to Quintly. Third-party sites also give more specific analytics on videos when they're natively hosted than they do for embedded YouTube videos.

8. Group Videos into a Series

By grouping your videos into a series by content theme, you create short, targeted video pieces (typically thirty seconds to two minutes) that tie together. This approach is helpful for your target audience, as they can jump around to exactly the content they need, rather than wade through a twenty-minute video for the portions that are relevant. A very popular use case is a series of product how-to videos that walk a customer or prospect through the process of using your product.

Video blogs, also known as vlogs, are similar in that they are typically grouped by date and searchable by topic. While vlogs are atypical for technical companies today, it is effective to mix in video content with written blog content to drive interest and test video adoption with your target personas.

9. Designate a Video Day

Staging a video with the proper lighting and audio components is time-consuming. Take full advantage of this effort by shooting as many videos as possible in one day. This also helps videos have a consistent look, feel and even spokesperson position from video to video. By designating a video day, you'll record more videos in less time, saving time and creating a library of content for months to come.

Final Checklist

- Script
- Spokesperson
- Production set – backdrop, lights, camera, microphone
- Video recording equipment
- Production software

Hiller Measurements hosts an interview-style video series called AE²: Artists, Engineers & Entrepreneurs

Creating a Low-Cost DIY Video Production Room

It's not difficult or expensive to transform a conference room or home office into a video production studio. Here is a gear shopping list:

- **Backdrop:** Opt for a conference room with light-colored walls and minimal background clutter ($0) or a solid screen kit ($140).

- **Lighting:** Use two to three bi-color dimmable LED softbox lights with stands to light the room and speaker ($100). Another option, at a very inexpensive price point, is to purchase clip lights at a hardware store ($15).

- **Camera and Tripod:** Smartphones such as the iPhone X and more recent versions rival their camera counterparts. If your smartphone shoots in 1080p, you are in good shape. You'll need a basic tripod to hold the phone at the perfect height and angle; a bonus feature is remote-triggered controls ($25).

- **Microphone:** Smartphone-compatible microphone options include lavalier microphones ($22 for two) and mounted shotgun directional microphones ($25), each of which plug into your phone's auxiliary port (with a converter for the iPhone).

- **Production Software:** Popular platforms include Apple's GarageBand (included with Mac computers) and Adobe Premiere Pro ($240).

Webinars

Like videos, webinars are highly educational recorded sessions. Unlike videos, which are typically used to provide a company overview or show a customer how a product works, webinars are more interactive, almost like a class. They typically include a speaker and a set of slides.

What Is a Webinar?

Webinars are long-form video content designed to educate the viewer about a central topic. A webinar can include a demo, but the focus should be on education, and the demo should fall at the end of the webinar.

- **Length**: Thirty to ninety minutes
- **Buyer's Journey Stage**: Identify (determine options for a solution, understand what's involved in obtaining the needed solution)
- **Cost to Reader**: Gated, premium content; viewers need to register and provide specific information to gain access
- **Life Span**: Up to two to three years
- **Time to Create**: Four to six weeks

Webinar Topics

- Industry trends
- Thought leadership
- Best practices
- How-to topics

Best Practices

Here are a few key considerations when creating this content:

1. Record Live and Offer On-Demand

Host a live webinar and then repurpose the recording as an on-demand webinar on your website. That on-demand webinar can be treated as a video for promotional purposes.

2. Consider the Length

Unlike video, longer is better for webinars. According to a study by GoToWebinar, webinars that are sixty minutes long attract 2.1 times as many registrants as thirty-minute webinars, and ninety-minute webinars attract 4.6 times as many.

3. Find a Partner

Consider partnering with another organization to increase your audience reach, boost participation, and reduce the workload for your company. This could be an industry peer, a customer, or a partner. Conducting a webinar together allows you to co-market and share audiences.

4. Interact During Live Webinars

If you're hosting a live webinar, interact with your viewers. Ask questions, conduct polls, and conclude with a survey to encourage participation.

5. Use a Moderator

Have an administrator or moderator help you navigate polls or audience questions throughout the webinar. This should not be any of the webinar speakers.

6. Promote It

Webinars are resource-intensive, and your audience needs advance notice to sign up and allot time for your webinar. Schedule it one to two months in advance and promote it once it's scheduled via social media, enewsletter, and blog.

Final Checklist

- Engaging title
- Slide deck with the right transitions between slides
- Polls or interactive content
- Script
- Moderator

Webinar promotional graphic used on website and in social channels.

White Papers and Ebooks

Technical audiences traditionally have considered white papers and ebooks as unbiased, lengthy academic articles that look like a chapter straight out of a textbook. However, white papers and ebooks have become a great media format in content marketing to attract and inform customers. They can teach or show thought leadership in technical areas.

What Are White Papers and Ebooks?

White papers are persuasive, authoritative, and in-depth content designed to explain a particular issue, topic, or technology and provide a methodology. Like a case study, a white paper addresses your target audience's pain points, but it goes deeper into explaining the research and proof points that support your methodology.

Featuring typically 1,800 to 2,400 words of dense content with few images, white papers generally contain diagrams and embedded videos and links. Given the amount of time it takes to create a white paper, you should choose an evergreen topic that is not tied to a specific date or time period. Write the content in a way that addresses common or recurring pain points for your potential customers.

Ebooks also feature in-depth content; however, they often cover more than one topic. Ebooks are educational PDF resources. Think of them as similar to white papers but covering more topics or examining the topic at hand much more deeply. An ebook typically follows the same process as a white paper but is three to four times longer and takes at least twice the effort to create. One way to create an ebook is to develop a series of white papers and then modify and combine them to compile a cohesive ebook.

- **Buyer's Journey Stage**: Explore (identify options for a solution, understand what goes into getting the solution you need); Evaluate (prove expertise so that the buyer can make a final purchase decision)
- **Length**: 1,800 to 2,400 words (white paper); 7,500 to 10,000 words (ebook)
- **Cost to Reader**: White papers take substantial time to create, and they are typically presented as gated content, or content that users must provide some information to get; because ebooks are longer, you can require more fields on the lead form, and buyers can expect to give more information to get the content they need to make a decision
- **Life Span**: White papers and ebooks typically have a shelf life of two to five years; again, depending on your industry, it's a good best practice to annually review white papers to ensure that the content and research are still up to date
- **Time to Create**: Four to six weeks for a white paper; six to eight weeks for an ebook

White Paper and Ebook Topics

- Introductory information about a technology
- How-to tutorials or best practices

- Authoritative reports about industry changes
- Lessons learned about an engineering challenge
- Analysis from your research and experience

Best Practices

Here are a few key considerations when creating this content:

1. Identify Customer Pain Points

The key to writing a good white paper is to put yourself in the reader's shoes and consider, "What does the customer want to learn?" However, the hook is just the first step to getting eyes on your article. Go back to this pain point when you're creating your paper title and introduction. If you can relate to the exact headaches and burdens your audience faces, you can immediately build the trust you need to keep your prospects reading.

2. Outline Your Paper

Committing 1,500 or more words to paper may seem overwhelming, so the best way to defeat writer's block is to create an outline. Do the structure and flow of the document make sense and drive to your key points and goals? Once you have established the framework of the white paper, organize your source material under each outline point and add extra notes and thoughts as they come to mind.

3. Research and Source Data

Technical audiences look for technical detail, so include appropriate references and links to other sites to increase the credibility and depth of your content.

4. Consider Visuals

Since white papers can be very text-heavy, keep the reader's interest visually by breaking up the content with quotes, callout text blocks, and enticing images. Label the pictures, diagrams, and tables with full-sentence descriptions that help summarize the content in case readers scan the material.

5. Use CTAs

No matter how educational or objective the white paper may be, remember to include CTAs, next steps, or related links you wish the reader to follow. You are not writing this white paper for free; it is intended to move people further through the buyer's journey.

6. Plan Ahead

Allow for time to create this lengthy content; it can often take up to six weeks to write and complete.

7. Avoid the Sales Pitch

White papers should be rich with information. They should show thought leadership or deep instruction without bombarding readers with a sales pitch. Content creators can subtly add a company logo to the paper design and offer more information on next steps with the company for readers who need more data after finishing the content. The best white papers are so compelling that readers want to interact with the company afterward because the material they read was so helpful. Readers will have greater trust in the company that offered the paper.

Final Checklist

- A table of contents if it's longer than five pages
- A bold title (e.g., controversy addressed, lessons learned) with emphasis on the first fifty-five characters so it will display well in search engines
- Descriptive text without industry buzzwords; spell out acronyms and initialisms on first reference
- Relevant imagery, diagrams, charts, or graphs
- An abstract and executive summary
- Cited data to support your point

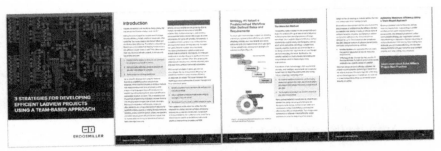

A technical white paper, complete with images.

Corporate Slide Decks

Corporate slide decks provide a branded foundation for all company overviews and presentations.

What Is a Corporate Slide Deck?

A corporate slide deck covers the foundational topics of a company, including the customer challenge the company solves and the types of results customers see after working with the company. The corporate slide deck should be a living document, updated and expanded over time. It often becomes a large deck with an arsenal of slides for different audiences, all branded with the same look and feel.

- **Length**: Fifteen to twenty slides
- **Buyer's Journey Stage**: Evaluate or Decide (in-person or virtual presentation, specific to the buyer's needs); Advocate (nurture existing customers, build brand awareness)
- **Cost to Reader**: N/A; typically presented to audience
- **Life Span**: Two to three years with annual updates
- **Time to Create**: Four to six weeks

Recommended Corporate Slide Deck Flow

- **Cover**: Make sure your title page is clean and clear; it should include your company's visual brand colors and logo and your company name and tagline.

- **Problem**: Define your customers' problems as they see them.

- **Amplify (Market Info)**: Dive into your customers' problems and show what will happen if those problems remain unaddressed. Use data if possible and show what kind of market potential customers will pass up if they don't solve the challenges their businesses face.

- **Solution (What We Do)**: Clearly state what you do and tie your solutions directly to the problems you identified on the second slide.

- **How We Work**: Show how you deliver the solutions that will meet your customers' needs. Include relevant leadership or company overview information.

- **Results**: Revisit the problem statements and show what customers can achieve by using your solutions. Quantify your results, if possible.

- **Who We Are**: Key leadership or account team introductions.

- **Partnerships/Certifications**: Highlight partnerships, certifications, and memberships that are particularly important to your customers.

- **Specialties**: Speak to any specific technology or application areas within your realm of experience.

- **Competitive Advantage**: Answer the questions your customers may have about alternatives to using your company but haven't had a chance to ask yet.

- **Next Steps**: End your presentation with a CTA. This may be contact information, your website, or an easy-to-remember URL that leads to follow-up content. Alternatively, this slide can be a transition into the remainder of a customized presentation.

Best Practices

Here are a few key considerations when creating this content:

1. Remember the Sales Process Has Changed

Even if you have a slide deck, it may need updating. As a vendor, your face-to-face interaction with a customer is being pushed later in the buyer's journey. Today's customers don't interact directly with a company until much of their research is complete and potential vendors are identified. Now, sales decks help to qualify leads who already know they have a challenge and are actively looking for a solution. Rather than try to prove to a customer that they need what you're selling, an effective deck relates to the potential customer's problem and positions a company's product or service as a trustworthy solution. The deck builds rapport.

2. Tell the Bigger Story

Instead of jumping into the specs of your product or a comparison, a planned, designed slide deck helps you tell the bigger story about your company and prove yourself as an expert in the field.

3. Tell the Same Story, Regardless of Presenter

When members of your engineering team or sales staff tell your story, they likely gravitate to specific aspects of your product or solution and base the way they tell the story on their personality. One of your lead engineers may be highly detailed and technical in explaining specs and leading theories, while another may be focused on market trends and conversation. These people and their insight are highly valuable, but for brand consistency, each team member needs the ability to tell the same story.

4. Record a Presentation of Your Deck as an Internal Reference

Leave talking points in the notes section of your corporate slide deck and record a member of your leadership presenting your slides (this can be a voiceover-slide-progression format, like a webinar). Make this recording available for internal access at all times so that staff can reference the core presentation and message in preparation for any presentations they may give. This recording is also excellent new-hire training material.

5. Create Visuals That Match Your Tone

You can take liberties with images and graphic elements, but choose a few style options and stick with them. This gives your brand and message a consistent feel. When you're deciding how to design your slides, consider your tone:

- A **formal tone** may have a white background with simple headlines, a clear image, and bullet points on each slide
- A **conversational tone** may have a few more colors with bold statements and infographic-style graphic elements
- A **technical tone** may focus on images of customer applications, technical diagrams, and bulleted technical details
- A **leadership tone** may include a full-bleed design, clean stock images, and industry data points

6. Give Your Sales Team a Tool and Templates as a Starting Point

Your engineering and sales presenters likely have slides full of data that they just love and that work effectively for them. Keep those slides but add them after the company overview and slightly modify them to match the corporate presentation.

Consider the types of slides your presenters frequently use and make templates for them. Typical templates in high demand include:

- Product family
- Product specs
- Industry experience
- Customer application

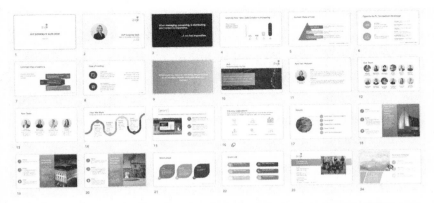

AVP's corporate slide deck balances educational content with interesting imagery. See more from AVP at weareavp.com.

Final Checklist

- Template with branded colors and logo
- Completed slides
- Extra templates for common slides your sales team needs
- Script or talking points
- Recorded presentation

Interactive Content

Think about the last time you took an online assessment or used a web-based calculator. You were probably engaged and learned something valuable.

According to Content Marketing Institute's (CMI) latest research, nearly half (46 percent) of marketers surveyed are using interactive content. Their top reason for doing so? Engagement followed by educating the audience, creating brand awareness, and generating leads.

What Is Interactive Content?

Interactive content requires participants' active engagement in addition to simply reading or watching. In return for that engagement, participants receive real-time, hyper-relevant results they care about.

Interactive content grabs attention and increases engagement, but it also takes more time and resources to design and build, so it's essential to think strategically about the kind of interactive content you will create.

- **Buyer's Journey Stage**: Evaluate (match needs with capability); Decide (provide ROI or cost of ownership data)
- **Cost to Reader**: Depending on the type of information, interactive content may be gated; see the first best practice below
- **Life Span**: Because it is often data-rich and needs to be heavily updated over time, interactive content usually lasts one to two years
- **Time to Create**: Eight to twelve weeks

Interactive Content Topics

- Interactive images
- Calculators
- Industry-specific diagrams
- Product configuration tools

Best Practices

Here are a few key considerations when creating this content:

1. Decide Whether to Use a Lead Form

Organizations can gate ROI calculators after prospects input their data and then send prospects the results of their calculations via email. Interactive graphics are not gated but used as a navigation tool to showcase other content or to make information discovery simple for prospects.

Below is an interactive product selection tool. This tool helps prospects easily find exactly what they need without a lead form.

2. Create Industry-Specific Diagrams

An easy way to showcase your technical expertise is with an interactive diagram that details a product, process, or application. Interactive diagrams can link to relevant content, such as case studies, white papers, ebooks, blog posts, or service pages.

Maury Microwave offers an Interactive Adapter Finder, helping web visitors to easily select products that meet their specifications.

Wineman Technology (WTI) uses interactive diagrams on web pages to help readers find relevant content. Visitors can scroll over different parts of an automobile or airplane to see components of test systems WTI has built. Each point on the diagram is linked to a relevant case study. By adding these interactive graphics to highly trafficked pages on

7. <u>Landing Gear Test System</u>
WTI has experience designing custom landing gear test systems for both components as well as complete landing gear.

WTI's interactive graphic shows the test system created for each part of the aircraft. The names of the test systems also link to more information on the specific application.

its website, WTI saw an increase in average time spent on these pages from less than one minute to more than two minutes.

3. Add Interactivity to Infographics

Interactive infographics take the power of the conventional infographic and add an element of dialogue between your brand and audience.

They require more resources than static infographics, yet they can increase traffic, SEO backlinks, and user engagement. If you already have an infographic designed and built, you can work with a web developer to transform your infographic to interact with users.

4. Create a Calculator

This form of interactive content consists of taking a user's input and, based on a formula, creating a numerical answer. Users value this tool because it can quickly convey factual data like ROI and total cost of ownership. The philosophy of a calculator is simple: no fluffy words, just pure data.

A calculator provides precise results that are suitable for complex strategies. Instead of writing a lot of content describing a product or service, you can create a calculator that offers an accurate output of the gains resulting from purchasing that product or service. Your prospects then know whether buying it is profitable.

Additionally, a calculator requires a small amount of effort from users but provides them with great value.

Final Checklist

- Determine desired user experience
- Map input/output parameters
- Design and program
- Launch on website

Podcasts

Over the past six years, podcasts have steadily grown in adoption. According to the 2019 Infinite Dial report by Edison Research and Triton Digital, podcasting reached a significant milestone in 2019 with the majority of Americans saying they have listened to at least one. Forty percent of those under twenty-four and 39 percent of those ages twenty-five to fifty-four listen to podcasts monthly, with adoption posting double-digit growth in 2019 over 2018. Podcast listeners in the U.S. averaged seven podcasts per week. These findings, coupled with audiobook adoption, shows a clear trend of increased spoken word audio consumption.

For technical businesses, podcasting represents a way to build thought leadership, demonstrate your expertise, and inspire customer loyalty.

It is common for busy professionals to consume audio content during long commutes or workouts on their smartphone, which is an important consideration when weighing format and publishing options.

What Is a Podcast?

Podcasts are focused pieces of audio content streamed or downloaded by the listener through their computer or smartphone. They are often published in a collection or series, connected by a common topic thread, which listeners subscribe to through a Podcast app.

B2B podcasts tend to be educational or inspirational in nature. The most common formats are interviews and subject-matter expert commentary. Similar to written blog posts, podcasts should be primarily educational, with very little directly promotional content.

- **Buyer's Journey Stage**: Explore (industry trends, best practices); Identify (thought leadership, how-to)
- **Length**: Long enough to cover the subject, but no longer (in other words, there is no hard and fast rule!); that being said, if you believe your target personas are listening on the go, consider maxing out at an average commute time of about twenty-two minutes
- **Cost to Listener**: Free or for a subscription
- **Life Span**: Two to three years
- **Time to Create**: One to two weeks

Podcast Formats

- Interview
- Commentary
- How-to

Best Practices

Here are a few key considerations when creating your podcast:

1. Choose a Format That Fits Your Needs

When establishing a podcast, you'll have some important decisions to make about format and cadence. Typical formats for B2B podcasts are:

- **Interview**: Within a predetermined theme (e.g., RF technology, system integration, cloud application security), the podcast host will interview different related experts. This style can save you time, as your guest is helping create the podcast content. It also provides the opportunity for you to expand your podcast reach through your guests' networks.

- **Commentary**: With this style, an SME is designated as the podcaster, and the podcast provides the means to educate and build thought leadership for both the SME and the company. This format is well suited to companies that already have an SME positioned as your company spokesperson (such as a CTO or Fellow).

- **How-to**: Instructional content is quite popular for engineers and could help you build a following quickly. The trick is to have topics that lend themselves to audio only, not needing video or other visual support to explain the content.

2. Choose a Cadence You Can Sustain

How often you podcast depends on your podcast goals and what is realistic with your bandwidth. Whatever cadence you do choose, you'll want to commit to so that your listeners know what to expect. Weekly may be too intensive to maintain, so perhaps start with a monthly podcast to get some traction going. Then, if this seems manageable, consider raising the frequency over time.

Another strategy is to record a whole podcast series and push all episodes at once. This has some upsides, as you can put more concentrated marketing effort towards the launch. Once attracting listeners, you can gain subscribers for future podcast series. At a minimum you'll want to post at least three episodes when launching your podcast. This will help attract subscribers and boost your download numbers (giving you a chance of being featured on Apple's New and Noteworthy list).

3. Leverage Low-Cost Tech to Produce Easier and Cheaper

Don't let the technical side seem like a giant hurdle. There are simple, low-cost tools you can use to produce a quality podcast. Here are the top items you'll need:

- USB microphone with pop filter, such as Blue Yeti
- Recording and editing software, such as GarageBand or Audacity
- Podcast host, such as Buzzsprout
- Transcription software, such as Scribie (to post a transcript to your website)

4. Avoid Word Vomit and Robotic Scripts

Your speaker should sound natural and engaging, and take pains to be succinct and to the point. If they ramble too much, particularly at the start, listeners may drop off early, and worse, not return for future episodes.

By outlining the material and practicing verbal delivery, your speaker will get a feel for timing and balance of material and be less prone to rambling. Scripting can take this process one step further, but beware of having the robotic tone of a stilted script reader rather than an approachable human.

5. Record and Edit

After recording your podcast, you'll move into the editing phase. Best practices for editing include:

- Separating material into an introduction, body content (which could be further broken into sections if the podcast is long), and a wrap-up
- Cutting out repetitious or rambling content
- Adding a catchy intro, with the podcast name and music
- Smoothing out the sound quality to avoid large variability in loudness

Pro tip: If your podcast is in interview format, and you plan to interview people remotely via an internet connection, consider using Zencaster. With this software platform, each speaker's audio is recorded locally on their computer, which maintains a higher quality recording by avoiding degradation caused by audio transmission over an internet connection. Once the recording is finished, the podcast editor can marry the two files during the editing process.

6. Provide Transcript and Additional Resources

Make it easy for your listener to simply listen to your podcast by providing them with the transcript and additional related resources on your website. This is not only a helpful service for the listener, who probably shouldn't be taking notes while on the freeway or gym treadmill, but helps you further engage them once they visit your website.

7. Brush Up on Podcasting Hosting Platforms' Launch Steps

When you are ready to launch your podcast, there are specific steps that need to be taken to be listed on the major podcast directories (e.g. Apple, Spotify, Google). With each, you'll need to set up your directory listing, complete with thumbnail artwork, a title, and an RSS feed to a

This interview-style podcast showcases new marketing and sales books with new episodes published biweekly.

hosting platform such as Buzzsprout, where your podcast content will live. Top hosting platforms have shortcuts to help ease the directory listing process, in addition to other features that make their low-cost subscription fee worth the investment.

Once your podcast is launched and listed in directories, follow the content promotion steps from Chapter 8 for attracting podcast subscribers.

Final Checklist

- Choose format and cadence
- Obtain production materials
- Outline your podcast material
- Record and edit your podcast
- Launch your podcast

Chapter 6
EDIT AND POLISH YOUR CONTENT

Once you've drafted your content, you still have a few more tasks before you can publish and promote it. You need to review your content with your SMEs (typically one review for blog posts and up to three reviews for intensive content like white papers or videos), edit your content, include images, and add CTAs.

CONTENT DEVELOPMENT TIMELINE: WHITE PAPER

Week	Writer	Subject Matter Expert (SME)	Designer
Before Beginning	Decide on content topic Decide on SME and notify of plans and expectations		
Week 1	Brainstorm outline Draft interview questions to gather information needed Interview SME Optional: Create outline and review with SME	Send any exisiting source material on the topic to writer	
Week 2	Write first draft		
Week 3	Discuss imagery options with SME	Review draft and provide feedback and additional technical detail where necessary	
Week 4	Write second draft, including images and captions where needed		Create white paper stemplate and any additional imagery needed
Week 5		Provide feedback on second draft	
Week 6	Create final draft		Complete layout and adds final draft text

Sample content development timeline for a white paper that involves a writer, an SME, and a designer.

Review Processes with SMEs

If you secured an SME commitment to help create a piece of content, make sure you follow through with a tight process and clear expectations. Set detailed timelines and ask for any conflicts such as travel or project deadlines they may foresee so you can adjust.

Each time you send a draft for review, let them know what you're looking for in return. Depending on content type and how much source material you have, the expectations for review are different, but here are some general expectations for an SME to review a white paper:

1. Stick to a Time Limit

A comprehensive white paper review takes sixty to ninety minutes. With a shorter review, you may not get the detail you need; with more time, your SME may rewrite sections or head down a rabbit hole with new details that may not fit your topic or audience.

2. Assess the Overall Framework

Determine if the topics are covered well and in the right order, as if you were having a casual conversation with a prospect. Edits at this point often include reordering a paragraph or suggesting different wording for a headline, subhead, intro, conclusion, or intro sentence for a section.

3. Review Technical Terms

Check for insider or industry terms that would better speak to the audience and your expertise. Edits here often look like simple changes to wording. For example, defining a company as ISO 9001 certified is more powerful than saying it has a quality management system. Or, the term IoT is commonly accepted by engineers and doesn't need to be spelled out as "Internet of Things." On the contrary, spelling it out on every reference makes you appear as if you don't fully understand your audience.

4. Evaluate the Accuracy of the Technical Details

Make sure you haven't missed an opportunity to provide a measurement or quick example to show value. For example, an engineer with knowledge of specific projects can replace "extreme temperatures" with "temperatures up to 130 degrees Fahrenheit," which immediately creates a clearer picture.

Edit Content

All your content needs to be edited before it's published. Glaring errors in grammar and flow diminish trust and make a brand seem rushed and sloppy.

Common Edits

Here's a list of common errors and issues in technical content:

1. Compound Adjectives/Modifiers

Generally, hyphenate two or more words when they precede the noun they modify and act as a single idea.

- **Incorrect**: the high frequency, easy to use oscilloscope
- **Revised**: the high-frequency, easy-to-use oscilloscope
- **Incorrect**: the new device is user-friendly
- **Revised**: the new device is user friendly

2. Overcapitalization

The names of industries and many technical terms that take acronyms don't need to be capitalized. Do a quick search to see if the term in question should be capitalized.

Example:

- I/O is the abbreviation for input/output. When spelled out, "input/output" does not need to be capitalized.

3. Abbreviations

Typically, you should spell out a term on first reference and enclose the abbreviation in parentheses. On all subsequent references, you can use the abbreviation.

Example:

- Content marketing (CM) is an important part of an overall marketing strategy. CM plans rely heavily on consistently published content.

4. Quotations

Use quotation marks when quoting directly, listing a title of a work, and implying alternate meanings. When using quotations, include punctuation before the end quotation mark.

Examples:

- We recently published a blog post, "Strategies to Control New Theories in Variable Valve Timing."
- Transitioning your company's computer workloads from an onsite host model to an internet, or "cloud-based" model can save tremendous time and money.

5. Overly Complicated Language

Technical content can get bogged down by wordy phrases. Consider these substitutes:

- During the course of → During
- In the form of → As
- In many cases → Often
- In the event of → If
- Exhibits the ability to → Can
- In order to → To
- Utilize → Use

6. Sentence Fragments

Make sure each sentence contains a grammatically complete, independent thought that stands alone.

Example:

- **Incorrect**: PXI instrumentation is modular by design. Although engineers can purchase complete systems.
- **Revised**: PXI instrumentation is modular by design, although engineers can purchase complete systems.

7. Misplaced Modifiers

Place modifiers adjacent to the words they describe to avoid changing the meaning of the sentence, and take care to ensure that the modified words actually appear in the sentence.

Example:

- **Incorrect**: The broken engineer's system is causing substantial downtime for overall production.
- **Revised**: The engineer's broken system is causing substantial downtime for overall production.

8. Faulty Parallelism

Be sure you use grammatically equal sentence elements to express two or more matching ideas or items in a series.

Example:

- **Incorrect**: The engineer's plans include designing a widget, a prototype, and deploying a complete solution.
- **Revised**: The engineer's plans include designing a widget, developing a prototype, and deploying a complete solution.

Note: This is important for lists of features or bullets. They are much easier to read if they hold the same structure (i.e., all bullets are phrases that start with a verb, or all bullets are adjectives, nouns, and so on).

9. Easily Confused Words

Watch out for words that sound the same but have different meanings when spelled differently.

Example:

Incorrect: The scientist choose not to give specific advise.

Revised: The scientist instructor chose not to give specific advice.

10. Units

Be careful with unit abbreviations. For example, kb and kB are completely different measurements (kilobit versus kilobyte). Do a quick Google search on units while editing to make sure any abbreviations are correct.

11. Passive Voice

Passive voice isn't an error, but excessive passive voice creates weak content. When you see passive voice, try to edit the sentence to remove it.

Example:

- **Passive voice**: New frequency ranges can be reached with the signal generator.
- **Active voice**: The signal generator reaches new frequency ranges.

Need help deciding if a technical term should be hyphenated or abbreviated? Do a quick Google search and evaluate how others use the term. Consider how it's used on Wikipedia and in major, respected publications and make a call from there.

Corporate Style Guides

In addition to typical spelling and grammar editing, you likely have words, phrases, acronyms, product names, and industry terms that you need to standardize. It's important to be consistent with these terms so your content maintains the same look and feel.

To ensure consistency across your company, start with *The Associated Press Stylebook* or *The Chicago Manual of Style* for a style reference and then consider establishing a company style guide to use on the next piece of content you edit. When you encounter a term that a variety of people in your company use differently, note it and decide how to universally use this term. For example, the military/aerospace/defense industry is labeled differently by different companies. Whether you use mil/aero or aero/defense isn't a huge issue, so long as you standardize to ensure that your content feels consistent and trustworthy.

Companies typically need to decide how to handle the following terms:

- Company name
- Product names (including product numbering)
- Industries
- Company initiatives and thought leadership areas

Lastly, a few final tips:

1. Don't Subvert Grammar or Style for a Company or Product Name

It's difficult to be consistent with product or company names that are all lowercase, capitalized, or italicized or that contain special symbols. Starting a sentence with a product name that must be all lowercase looks out of place. It's unfamiliar to readers and visually displeasing, causing them to pause. That said, your logo can use all lowercase letters; just don't write your product name that way in text.

2. Don't Abbreviate Terms That Are Important for Branding or SEO

If you're still developing your brand, don't rush to abbreviate your company name or terms that you're using to try to position yourself as an expert. For example, if your company is called Medical Instrumentation, the name alone gives a great idea of what your company does.

Don't rush to abbreviate your company name to "MI." It will take years for customers and prospects to know your company and brand well, and it's helpful for them to see and hear your full name as often as possible at the start.

Imagery

The effective use of graphics can immediately grab users' attention, communicate to your audience what you stand for, and present your company's personality.

In addition, imagery SEO applied correctly on your website can boost your search engine ranking and attract new organic visits to your website.

But like all things web, there is a right way to implement images for success and effectiveness. When placing graphics on your website to better reach your audience and drive traffic and clicks, follow these guidelines:

1. Use Meaningful, High-Quality Imagery

As soon as visitors land on your website, they should be able to tell what your company is about and how it serves them. Incorporate meaningful, impactful images in the homepage and other landing pages so visitors immediately understand the purpose of your site and click through to learn more.

2. Use Stock Imagery Sparingly and Carefully

Do your best to select stock photos that relate as much as possible to your applications and industries. Generic stock imagery of businesspeople sitting in a meeting room, for example, turns visitors off to your site and doesn't say anything about who you are. Use very specific, long-tail keywords when searching stock imagery sites to find the best images for your needs. Also, work with a graphic designer who can recommend the right stock images for the dimensions of your site's layout.

3. Incorporate Graphic Icons for Better Web Usability

According to usability experts at the Nielsen Norman Group, icons have many benefits. They are quickly recognized at a glance and visually pleasing, they save space, and they support the notion of a product family when the same icons are used in several places.

Use simple graphic icons to break up text when there are many paths to choose from, such as on your homepage or service and solutions pages.

Hallam-ICS uses icons to quickly communicate business focus areas.

4. Enhance Scanning with Smart Imagery in Body Text

It's no secret that web visitors read only 20 percent of the text on the page, and the eye tends to linger on images more than text. Why not incorporate more graphic elements within your body text to facilitate scanning and quick comprehension of content?

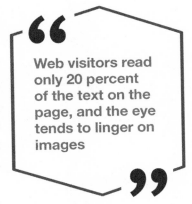

Web visitors read only 20 percent of the text on the page, and the eye tends to linger on images

Section Three

Publish and Promote Your Content

Chapter 7
WHERE AND HOW TO PUBLISH

Congratulations! You have defined and prioritized your audience personas, crafted your company narrative, developed your content plan, and begun creating optimized content at a steady cadence. Content marketing is a big investment, and you want to do all you can to maximize your return. Your prospects and customers need to find your content, read your content, and take appropriate action.

This section focuses on how to make your packaged pieces of content accessible to your target personas, tactics to help them find your content (hello search engine optimization!), and ways to entice them to read your content.

Chapter 8 starts with the important role of your website and your ability to support marketing technology. Then it provides a helpful way to assess your current state. You'll learn about the different types of web content and take a deeper dive into the more specialized layouts and functionalities that are game changers for your content marketing program.

Once you move into chapter 9, you'll learn how engineers seek out information to make a purchase decision and walk through the major promotional channels ideally suited for content marketing.

This chapter, 7, primarily focuses on the various methods of publishing content on your company website. It also discusses how to optimize your content for search during the publishing process and dives into best practices for creating landing pages with forms. Printed collateral form factors and best practices round out the publishing topics.

Prepare to Publish with a Technology Assessment

To efficiently implement your content marketing strategy, you should consider software to be your best friend. Marketing technology (martech) encompasses an array of software tools that help you publish content, capture and nurture leads, pass qualified leads to sales, and measure results.

What Is in Your Martech Stack?

A suite of such software tools is often referred to as your "martech stack," and it includes your website content management system (CMS), customer relationship management (CRM) system, marketing automation, document management system (DMS), and specialized functional software tools. Some platforms also serve as supporting technology for sales, particularly CRM systems. Ideally, marketing and sales work within one unified tool, or

Ideally marketing and sales work within one unified tool so that both have access to buyer's journey intelligence.

they at least have tools that integrate, so that both groups have access to intelligence gathered throughout the buyer's journey.

These software tools typically offer the following features and benefits:

Content Management System (CMS)

- Easily add, remove, and update web pages and web content within a page
- Post new blogs and easily edit past blogs
- Manage on-page SEO
- Incorporate features, such as e-commerce and customer portals, often through third-party add-ons or APIs
- Provide web reporting

Customer Relationship Management (CRM) System

- Single-source repository for all contacts your company interacts with, from prospects to customers

- Sales tools for prospecting and opportunity management
- Lifecycle and lead stage tracking
- Sales reporting

Marketing Automation (MA) Software

- Email marketing
- Social media management
- Lead scoring
- Automated workflows for external communications and internal processes and alerts
- Marketing reporting

Document Management System (DMS)

- Central repository of documents
- Potential use by all or specific functional divisions, depending on company size
- Content grouping by topic or function
- Internal workflows and communication regarding specific content pieces
- Content utilization reporting

Functional Software Tools

- E-commerce
- Social media management
- SEO
- Chatbots
- Account-based marketing
- Digital advertising
- Analytics
- Video hosting and analytics

Some software platforms, such as HubSpot, combine many of these functions into one integrated experience and connect to specialty tools via APIs. Other software platforms focus on one particular function (e.g., WordPress for web, Hootsuite for social, Google Analytics for measurement, Drift for chatbots, Terminus for account-based marketing, and so on).

Use the following questions to assess whether you have gaps in your martech stack:

- Can you easily publish and update content on your website?

- Is your website structure sound? Is it responsive, secure, and does it load quickly?

- Do your target personas think your website is easy and intuitive to navigate?

- Does your website contain a blog?

- Can you serve up content within context? This context might be in the form of past downloads, pages visited, demographic information collected, etc.

- Can you easily create landing pages with forms, and do you have an automated way to store contact information and process content requests?

- Can you manage your contacts' communication preferences within the confines of privacy laws?

- Can you pass leads to sales efficiently and close the loop on lead interactions over time?

- Can you quickly measure KPIs to determine the effectiveness of your content marketing program?

If you answered no to any of these, you may need to add or upgrade your software tools.

As you do, strongly consider a platform that provides a holistic view of your content marketing programs by integrating sales and marketing functions. With an integrated approach, you can:

- Use intelligence from a prospect's activity to tailor content and communication
- Monitor when a prospect is ready to have a sales discussion
- Prioritize follow-up activity based on who is likely to buy
- Work efficiently and save money by having fewer tools to learn and manage
- Measure how activities led to a closed won sale
- Foster sales and marketing alignment

Is Your Website Healthy?

Your website is the very first and *most important* place you will publish your content because this is where your prospects will go first to find information. The number one source engineers use to seek information is vendor websites. That is very encouraging news! However, 55 percent of visitors spend less than fifteen seconds deciding whether to stay on your website. How does your website fare?

Think carefully about the implications of this for your content marketing strategy: In a nutshell, this reveals a few quick facts. People generally don't have enough patience to read through your content until they are initially engaged. If they deem the content valuable and from a reputable source, they are willing to invest more time. If your content appears too long, they may not bother giving it a chance. Also, technical web factors many marketers don't consider as part of their content strategy, such as site speed, matter a great deal to both users and search engines.

According to the Nielsen Norman Group, experts in research-based web usability, the top four factors for establishing trust within your website have remained stable over the years despite changing trends:

1. Design quality—organization, color scheme, and imagery

2. Up-front disclosure and transparency

3. Comprehensive, correct, and current content

4. Connectivity to external sources

You might be cringing right now thinking about your site. Perhaps your website originated as a pet project by a staff software engineer with extra time, or maybe it was built before 2010. Maybe it takes an act of Congress

Here are table stakes for a healthy website:

- Modern and aesthetically pleasing

- Easy for your target personas to search and navigate

- Easy for you to update content frequently

- Fast at loading (less than three seconds on computers, less than one second on mobile devices)

- User friendly with imagery and small blocks of text

- Secure through SSL, which is a secure protocol that works on top of HTTP (Hypertext Transfer Protocol) to provide security; the acronym for both working together is HTTPS (Hypertext Transfer Protocol Secure)

- Responsive and adaptable so it displays optimally regardless of device type (e.g., desktop, tablet, mobile phone)

to update web content, or you are invisible on search. If any of this sounds like your website, you definitely need to take action *now* to redesign!

Template-based websites are wildly popular with small and medium sized businesses (SMB) because of their low cost of entry and ease of use. Popular website builder platforms include WordPress, HubSpot, Wix, Big-Commerce, Weebly, and Squarespace. Whichever platform you choose, be sure your website meets the table-stake requirements listed above to provide a solid platform for publishing your content.

Web Publishing

Now that we've identified the tools you need and the main functionality to look for, let's explore the various methods to publish content on your company website.

A website has many different flavors. Most sites use a set of templates that dictate the various design layout options. Midmarket websites commonly use five to ten templates within a site theme. Here are examples of how templates might be applied:

- **Template 1**: Homepage
- **Template 2**: Products/solutions/services family page
- **Template 3**: Specific products/solutions/services page
- **Template 4**: Flexible content page for about us, other similar free-flowing pages
- **Template 5**: Leadership team

Additionally, most websites contain a blog and landing pages (with forms) that have their own unique design layouts.

Why is this important? As you create new content, you need to know which template best suits the material and construct your content, images, and layout to meet your website's established template standards.

Pillar Pages

In chapter 1, you learned how search has evolved toward relational content. In chapter 3, you discovered how to map content relationships through a planning process called topic clustering. With this knowledge under your belt, you are ready to create pillar pages.

Pillar pages are long-form web page templates that cover your content theme thoroughly while linking to internal and external content that dives deeper into various topics. Think of this page as the hub of all information related to your theme, and the spokes are links to each topic.

By publishing content from your topic cluster and linking to the different content pieces through a pillar page, you demonstrate to both your site visitors and Google that you are an expert in a subject. With broad, comprehensive overview content focused on a subject and coupled with links to more in-depth content, pillar pages can help your web-

Pillar pages demonstrate your expertise in a subject.

site rank higher with search engines. In addition, well-constructed pillar pages are filled with calls to action for landing pages (with forms), which helps convert visitors to leads.

Industries, product families, application expertise, and technology trends are all worthy themes to consider when selecting a pillar page focus area.

To build a pillar page, first select a topic cluster (for a refresher on topic clusters, see chapter 3). Next, plan the construction of your pillar page. Make sure to comprehensively cover your theme along the buyer's journey through links to subtopics, and stay mindful of what your buyer personas are likely seeking when they visit the page. Topic content is often a mixture of blog posts, case studies, videos, infographics, product pages, and more. A typical pillar page construct looks like this:

- Brief introduction that speaks to your persona's needs and pain points
- Compelling imagery and visual elements for quick scanning, such as icons
- One case study
- One piece of lead-generating content
- FAQs, linking to blog posts covering each topic
- An offer or next step to increase conversion for visitors who are ready to speak to sales

As you build the page, link to each topic's page, blog post, or landing page and ensure that each content piece reciprocates by linking back to the pillar page. Examples include an FAQ section that links to related blog posts with answers to the questions and lead-generating content such as white papers.

Though pillar page design has no set rules, be sure these pages stand out visually and follow usability best practices. High-quality content should be the main focus, and pictures and graphics are great tools to visually engage visitors and break up blocks of text.

Gated material should have special treatment on the pillar page, including elements such as images and thoughtful placement, to encourage visits and lead conversions.

Blogs

Blogs are an essential part of a content marketing strategy. You can use them to publish fresh content on a regular basis, which has many benefits. Blogging

Qosina's pillar page provides diverse resources for design engineers who need to adhere to the ISO 80369 standard.

allows you to stay top of mind with prospects during a long sales cycle by adding
education and hence value for your customers. If done right, blogs help to boost
your SEO rankings. HubSpot's research
shows that B2B companies that blog generate 67 percent more leads than companies that don't. The research also shows
that companies that prioritize blogging
are thirteen times more likely to see positive ROI.

B2B companies that blog generate 67% more leads than companies that don't.

To build a blog following, you need to post on a regular basis. By
following a predictable publishing routine, you are not only providing
more helpful content to your audience and encouraging them to re-engage but also producing more content that points back to your site for
new visitors. Search engines re-index your site when new content is
published, which is another excellent reason to commit to a publishing cadence.

Choose a frequency and stick with it. We recommend a minimum
of three posts per quarter and, ideally, one to two posts per week.
The more frequently you blog, the more often you're reminding blog
subscribers to visit your site and share your information with others.
Choose a practical schedule, though. If the quality of your content is
poor because you don't have time to write effective posts, you do more
harm than good.

If you are struggling to meet your blogging frequency goals, try these
hacks to work smarter, not harder:

- Invite guests to contribute blogs on relevant topics
- Reference external blog posts, particularly on industry trends, new products, and other news-related topics
- Refresh older blog posts and repost (more on this tactic below)

As you draft your blog post for publishing, consider creating a mini "blog ad" image embedded within the blog post that incorporates a relevant visual and the title of the post. You will learn in chapter 9 that this image helps draw the eye when sharing blogs socially and helps drive traffic to the blog.

If you are already an active blogger, spend time reviewing your top twenty most popular blog posts. Make sure each has a blog ad image and call-to-action button. TREW took this action and saw a 74 percent increase in leads in just one quarter!

If your company has been blogging for several years at a fairly high frequency, you are a great candidate for a tactic

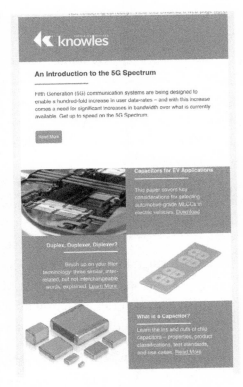

Knowles Precision Devices' ad promotes their capacitor fundamentals blog series.

known as historical blog optimization. This blogging strategy involves refreshing your content so that it is up to date and contains compelling calls to action, with the goal of attracting higher traffic and lead conversions.

The best way to optimize your historical blogs is to compile a report of blog posts with the highest views. These are your most valuable blog posts because they rank the highest in search and serve as the main attractors of visitors to your site. Prioritize your time here first and then look for blog posts that have a decent number of views but low conversions. These are your tier-two priority posts.

With your analysis and prioritization behind you, you can optimize and republish these blog posts.

For each post, review the content for outdated information, such as statistics, reports, and links. You also might need to update the introduction and conclusion of a post if they're no longer relevant. Because blogs are often dated, this date shows up in the meta description. Just by updating the date, you can increase the number of people who click on your blog.

Don't forget to update graphics and images in your blog posts if they've become outdated or don't best reflect your brand. Update calls to action in your post to promote new pieces of content you may have now. Even if you keep a call to action to the same landing page, you may want to redesign its graphic to increase clicks.

After you've optimized your old blog post, unpublish your original blog post and then republish it with a new date. It should take only an hour or two to complete these updates. Perhaps make a goal of tackling

Work Smarter, Not Harder: Historical Blog Optimization

TREW Marketing fully embraced the content marketing methodology of publishing blogs weekly (at first) and then later doubled down to twice weekly. Traffic showed nice year-over-year growth but not nearly at the same rate as the doubled time investment.

Upon analysis, the TREW team found that out of more than 600 blog posts over a decade, the top five performing blog posts received 650 times more views than the average TREW blog post and were all more than two years old.

With this analysis, team members decided that instead of continuing to create new blog posts twice weekly, their time would be better spent in updating the highest-performing blog posts that were generating the most organic search traffic and highest conversions.

The TREW Crew cut its overall time spent on blogging by 50 percent and experienced a 23 percent increase in blog views. Now that is working smarter, not harder!

one to three blog posts per week until you've worked your way through the entire list. Moving forward, review your blog metrics quarterly to identify any movement in your top blog list, which is a flag that you have new posts to update.

One last note: The blog area of your website is, or will be, a major contributor toward your overall site's search performance. Do not host your blog outside your domain or you will lose out on this boost and weaken usability for your target personas.

Landing Pages

The words "landing page" are used to describe a page with a form containing an overview of a content asset. These are the gateways to capturing new contacts and leads from your website.

Crank Software's ebook landing page is constructed for optimal performance.

You may be wondering when it's appropriate to gate content, or you may have concerns about gating your content given engineers' propensity toward privacy. I can share with certainty that engineers *will* fill out forms *if* the content offering is compelling. As discussed in chapter 2, the piece needs to be technical, meaty, and nonpromotional in nature.

Typical gated content includes white papers, webinars, and ebooks. Another gated content option might be a collection of several content pieces grouped together.

The key elements of a well-constructed landing page are:

- A short overview and the benefits the content offers
- A bulleted list of the contents, just detailed enough to entice visitors to download content without overwhelming them
- A picture of the cover of the content piece
- No global site navigation bar to improve page retention
- Short length of five fields or less
- Prominent call-to-action button

Our research shows that engineers are willing to provide personal details in exchange for valuable content, but there is a limit to how much you can ask. As shown by the following findings, engineers are

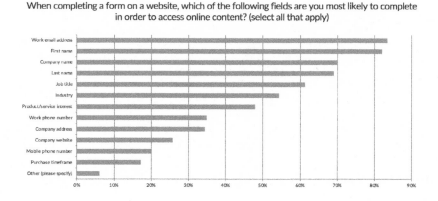

When completing a form on a website, which of the following fields are you most likely to complete in order to access online content? (select all that apply)

Engineers are most likely to fill out five form fields or fewer.

most likely to provide their names, company names, and work email addresses. Many respondents also provide industry and product and service interests.

Progressive profiling, or "smart forms," may be used to collect additional information with each new content download. Be sure all your forms comply with any applicable privacy laws whenever you are collecting, saving, and using a visitor's personal information. See sidebar on data privacy for more details.

Popular marketing automation platforms, such as HubSpot and Marketo, offer easy-to-use templates for landing page setup. Even if your website is housed in a different platform, you can skin these landing pages to look exactly like your website. This means that the header, footer, and basic design elements such as color and font are consistent with the rest of your website. By utilizing your marketing automation platform, the leads captured on your form automatically flow into your contacts database.

Once visitors complete your landing page form, they should be able to instantly access the piece of content. You can ensure this by redirecting them to a thank you page with a link, a redirect to a PDF, or an automated email with an email attachment. Your marketing automation system likely provides you with easy options for content delivery. If you create a page linking to the resource, take care to mark the page as non-indexable so that search

When web visitors request Vertech's Risk Mitigation Techniques white paper, they are offered a second, related white paper in the thank you email.

engines do not find the page—because if they can, visitors could theoreti-cally find and download the resource, bypassing the form altogether.

No matter how you share the content resource, always send your leads a follow-up email thanking them for completing a form. With marketing automation, you can easily send this email automatically using a workflow. Typically, the email includes a brief thank you, a link to the piece of content that the user downloaded from your landing page, and additional relevant content offers that help your new contact move through the buyer's journey.

Contextual Web Content

Picture in your mind a website that you often frequent. Does the company do anything to demonstrate that it remembers you on each visit? This might come in the form of a greeting with your name, auto-filling forms, or tailored shopping information based on your past orders.

This personalized experience is a type of contextual marketing. You serve up individualized web experiences to visitors based on their needs and preferences and store them in your CRM and marketing automation tools.

For example, let's say you'd like to take one of your solutions pages and tailor it toward an engineer specifier. Your standard page that everyone sees may have more benefits-oriented language, but the second version offers more in-depth technical details.

According to a study by Evergage and Researchscape, 98 percent of marketers agree that contextual marketing helps advance customer relationships. Top benefits cited include delivering a better customer experience, increasing loyalty, and generating a measurable ROI lift. Also, 90 percent of marketers noted a measurable improvement in their marketing results from contextual marketing tactics, and the vast majority plan to maintain or increase contextual marketing investment in the future.

Though this style of web marketing is more common in the B2C market and e-commerce-oriented B2B companies, and is usually very expensive to implement, the landscape is changing. Marketing automation and e-commerce platforms offer contextual marketing tools as part of their suite of features, making this type of marketing more approachable for the middle-market B2B company.

Marketers are implementing contextual marketing today in the following ways:

In which of the following digital channels are you using personalization?

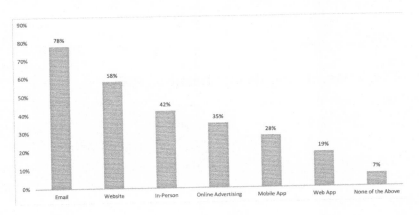

The top channels for contextual marketing experiences (Evergage 2019 Trends in Personalization Survey Report).

Some tactics, such as email tokens and progressive profiles (a.k.a. smart forms), are fairly simple and quick to implement. Other initiatives, such as customized web pages, require thoughtful planning and a robust database for accurate segmentation. The following few contextual marketing tactics are simple and quick. Start here and then adopt more sophisticated tactics once you establish your content marketing foundation and it is producing good results.

Simple contextual marketing tactics are a good place to start. They include:

- Email tokens, such as contact name, company name, and company description
- Smart web forms
  - Ability to autofill with known information
  - Progressive forms that ask for something new with each new form
  - GDPR compliance (see example below)
- Content delivery, offering a link to a resource for emails that show "undeliverable" in your database
- Smart calls to action based on previously seen web pages

On-Page Search Engine Optimization (SEO)

As you publish new content online, a key step is to optimize it for search. On-page SEO makes your web content easy to find by indexing it for search engines. This is done primarily through metadata and links.

Back when search engines were new on the scene (anyone remember Netscape and AltaVista?), marketers stuffed their web content with keywords and links to compel search engines to place them at the top of the search engine results page (SERP). Traditional SEO goals consisted of being found online and getting clicks. Traffic was key and lead

This form includes GDPR compliance language for web visitors with an EU IP address.

generation was an afterthought. In other words, the creation and manipulation of content trumped what site visitors actually wanted to read.

Today, 87 percent of the U.S. search engine traffic—and more than 90 percent of that of the top-GDP nations—flows through Google. The company is on a mission to provide authentic, contextual results to searchers. Google is not fooled by keyword manipulation. With machine learning such as Google's RankBrain, search engines associate past searches with similar topics and phrases to find the best search results. This change significantly improves search results for users and brings more *qualified* prospects to your website.

By authentically creating and publishing content based on your expertise in a consistent cadence, you are already well on your way to SEO nirvana. That said, you should take some additional technical steps periodically to help your website handshake with search engines and improve in SERP rankings. And if you skip these steps, no matter how great your content is, your site may as well be invisible to search engines, which will throw a big wrench into business goal achievement.

> Google is on a mission to provide authentic, contextual results to searchers.

Let's walk through how to optimize new content published to your website and how to improve your on-page SEO regularly.

Optimize New Web Content

As you post new web content on your site, you need to perform some SEO must-do tasks for each web page:

1. Authentically Include Keywords

Google and other search engines penalize your web page if the keyword density is over 2 percent (i.e., the same word is repeated throughout the web page), so don't overuse your focused keyword. If you have 300 words on your web page, use your keyword three to four times to meet the perfect keyword density percentage.

2. Don't Be Too Brief

SEO is all about proving to search engines that you are a trusted resource on a keyword and topic. Search engines track how many words are on your web pages. Demonstrate that you are an authority on your topic by including at least 300 words on each page.

3. Create Page Titles

Page titles (also known as title tags) appear in search engines and the web browser's title bar. They are given more weight in search engines than the actual headline of your web page (known as an H1 Header). Your title tags should be fifty-five characters or less because Google cuts off titles longer than this, and you'd like as much of your title to be visible as possible. Place the most important keyword early in your page title and use the word only once. Moz, an authority in all things SEO for B2B, recommends this structure: primary keyword - secondary keyword | brand name.

Example:

Computational Fluid Dynamics | MSI

Hold up, what is this H1 Header business? The very top-level headline of your web page is known in technical web terms as the H1 Header. One of the "early days" SEO tricks was for companies to stuff these headers with keywords. Search engine companies caught on, of course, and their algorithms have evolved to the extent that these are either weighted lightly or completely disregarded for SERPs. They are important to your site visitors, however, because they set the topic for the page. These too should be short and contain your primary keyword.

4. Create Meta Descriptions

Meta descriptions should be under 155 characters, again, because our friends at Google cut off longer content. This blurb should include a primary keyword and provide a compelling overview of the content that users see when they click through to the page.

5. Write Alt Text for All Images

Using alternative text helps search engines understand the context of any images, ranking them in image search for related terms and topics.

6. Create an Optimized URL

Include the key term toward the start of the URL, stick to a consistent structure, and use a relevant folder structure to help search engines understand where a page sits in your web hierarchy. For example, look at LHP Engineering Services' "About Us" page. The structure is reflected in the URL: https://lhpes.com/about-lhp.

7. Add Internal and External Anchor Links

As a marketer, you want visitors to view as many pages on your site as possible. To do this, add links to relevant blog posts and resources for visitors to continue reading and learning. You also want to link to external content when relevant. This not only creates a better user experience but also establishes a link back to your site (and search engines reward you for creating these associations).

8. Perform Routine On-Page SEO Improvements

Best-in-class marketers try to continually improve their on-page SEO by devoting time monthly to monitor SEO metrics and make technical improvements. Using an SEO diagnostic tool, such as Screaming Frog, Ahrefs, or Majestic SEO makes this work easier. You receive a report that lists all the pages on your website, including metadata, and raises flags when attention is needed.

Typical Routine On-page SEO Include the Following:

- **Update Metadata**: If you see dated or missing page titles, meta descriptions, or metatags, you can typically update these easily within your website's content management system.

- **Review and Refresh Top-Performing Content**: Check your analytics to see which web pages and blog posts are driving the most traffic to your site. Then check the publish date. Chances are the content is more than a year old and could use a critical review. This is a great opportunity to update the content with new data, fresh calls to action, and links to newer pages that expound on the topic. Whatever you do, *do not* archive the page or change the URL, no matter how outdated the material is. You do not want to lose the SEO gold you've created. Update the content, note the date it was updated, and republish.

- **Fix Broken Links**: Links are one of the biggest factors in Google's super-secret ranking algorithm, and they are worthy of your time. Use your SEO diagnostic tool to run a report of all links inside and outside your website, including those that are broken. Go through and update all broken links in your website; your site visitors will thank you! As for the external links (links from other websites), the work is a little harder because it requires reaching out to that organization's webmaster or marketing department and asking for a fix. Prioritize sites that are most relevant and strategic to your business and have high traffic and domain authority.

- **Resolve 404 Errors**: These pages are no longer active on your site; maybe they were deleted, unpublished, or not included in your last site design refresh. Set up redirects for these pages, pointing to live pages that fill the same need as the missing pages. This has the double benefit of boosting your SEO and providing a better user experience to anyone trying to visit those pages.

Ultimately, remember that SEO is for people, not search engines. Optimize your web pages and content to entertain and educate your visitors first. Use these SEO best practices to establish your site as a topic authority and create a better user experience.

SEO is for people, not search engines.

Printed Collateral: To Print or Not to Print?

The use of print collateral such as brochures and flyers has declined significantly in the past few decades to the point where some companies have done away with them altogether. They are mostly still found at trade shows, during "screenless" sales visits to highly secure locations or with high-level decision makers, and in computerless environments.

Printed materials can be costly and time-consuming to produce, and they quickly become outdated. Not only that, if you don't replicate the effort online, you miss the opportunity to reach a much greater number of buyers and improve your SEO performance. Think of how many flyers you've received at trade shows that you promptly threw in the trash bin instead of your suitcase for your flight home.

Rather than linger in "do what we've always done" mode, put yourself in the shoes of your top personas. Do you think they are more likely to consult a printed datasheet or search online for your product specs? I recall a story from one of TREW's clients about a company CEO who routinely took catalogs and printed lit as reading material on his flights, so he wanted the same produced for his company. The logic was flawed because the company did not target seventy-two-year-old company leaders; its audience was thirty-two-year-old engineer specifiers.

If you are planning to produce printed collateral, make sure you create useful pieces that stay current and enhance your brand by following these best practices.

Print Collateral Best Practices

The most common types of collateral are corporate brochures and flyers, and the latter is often referred to as a datasheet for product companies. Brochures are typically one, four, or eight pages with content on both sides of each page. Flyers and datasheets are typically one page and double-sided.

Start by thinking about how many collateral pieces you need, the purpose for each, and how they will work together. For instance, you will likely display all the pieces together at an event or customize a group of pieces for a sales visit. A common pairing for the latter is a corporate brochure with specific product or solution brochures tucked inside. Using a top- or side-tab color bar helps by providing a visual distinction for each flyer.

Hire or resource a designer to create collateral templates that can be applied to each printed piece. This ensures consistency between pieces and improves efficiency in layout. It is important to balance content, imagery, and white space. Blocks of text should be brief, and visual elements such as icons, diagrams, and specification tables should help the reader quickly scan and find information. Use columns to visually break up a page and mix different content elements together.

The design of your collateral pieces should be consistent with your company's visual identity and perhaps even mimic your website to a large degree. Don't forget to include your company logo, website, and phone number. These elements are often built into footers set apart visually from the rest of the piece.

> **Collateral templates ensure consistency and improve efficiency.**

Lastly, don't forget to include a visible call to action related to the collateral piece that drives the reader to your website to learn more and take the next step. You can use Bitly to create a very short URL for the purpose, which increases the likelihood that the contact actually visits the call-to-action URL. QR codes are also sometimes used; however, market adoption is low for these, so stick with a short URL instead.

Content Reuse

Core content is usually developed first and then leveraged in supporting pieces. For example, you may start with a white paper, which you then break up into multiple blog posts and repackage into a recorded webinar. Then perhaps you'll create promotional content, such as web pages, social media posts, enewsletter articles, and contributed article abstracts, to drive traffic to the white paper.

Another approach is to start with smaller content pieces, such as a collection of blog posts, and then package those into a meaty core content piece.

CONTENT REUSE

Start with a meaty content piece and repurpose the material into shorter content types.

Publishing Shortcuts

You can sort your content in two buckets:

- Core content (meaty, long-form pieces)
- Promotional content (shorter; often designed to promote core content)

The following content types work well as core and promotional content that targets technical audiences. Note that several content types can work as both primary and supporting pieces.

Core vs. Promotional Content

Content Type	Core	Promotional
Blog Post	✓	✓
Brochure	✓	✓
Web Page	✓	✓
Ebook	✓	
Case Study	✓	
Video	✓	✓
CAD Drawing	✓	
Presentation	✓	✓
White Paper	✓	
Infographic		✓
Social Media Posts		✓
Interactive Graphics		✓
Configurator/Calculators		✓
Datasheet	✓	
Evaluation Kit	✓	
Online Demo	✓	
Podcast	✓	
ENewsletters		✓

Some content types are core, original pieces while others can be either original or promotional in nature.

Quick Reference to Navigate Publishing Options

You may feel overwhelmed by the many different publishing options to consider while pinpointing which ones are the right fit for your content. Use this quick reference to determine where to publish by content type:

Starting Point for Publishing Content

Content Type	Form Factor
Application Expertise	Pillar Page
Company News	Blog Or Web Page
Forms	Contextual Web Content
Homepage	Template Web Page, Possible Contextual Web Content
How-To Video	Blog And On Youtube
Industry Page	Pillar Page
Product Family Expertise	Pillar Page
Product Overview And Specs	Product Web Page, Printed Collateral
Product Page	Template Web Page, Possible Contextual Web Content
Video	Embedded On Web Page Or Blog Post And On YouTube
Webinar	Landing Page With Form, Leading To A Link Sharing Pdf
White Paper	Landing Page With Form, Leading To A Link Sharing Pdf

Publishing options by content type.

Chapter 8
SHARE YOUR CONTENT

You've worked diligently to create and publish high-quality content. Now is not the time to "set it and forget it." You need to use a diverse set of channels to help engineers find and consume your information. This chapter presents the most effective promotional channels along each stage of the buyer's journey.

Where to Promote Content

You can choose from many promotional channels, each with a varying level of cost, effort, and predictability for positive outcomes. Research findings, past experience, and testing can all help inform which channels work best for reaching technical audiences.

The following chart shows the results of a research study in which engineers were asked which media sources they value most when seeking information.

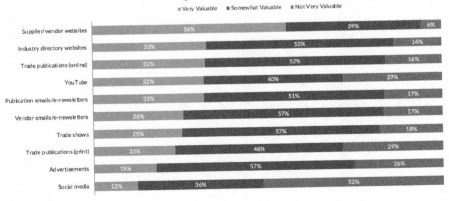

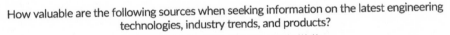

How valuable are the following sources when seeking information on the latest engineering technologies, industry trends, and products?

	Very Valuable	Somewhat Valuable	Not Very Valuable
Supplier/vendor websites	56%	39%	6%
Industry directory websites	33%	53%	14%
Trade publications (online)	32%	52%	16%
YouTube	32%	40%	29%
Publication emails/e-newsletters	32%	51%	17%
Vendor emails/e-newsletters	26%	57%	17%
Trade shows	25%	57%	18%
Trade publications (print)	23%	48%	29%
Advertisements	18%	57%	26%
Social media	12%	36%	52%

Engineers value supplier/vendor websites, search engine results, and technical publications most as sources of content. 2020 Smart Marketing for Engineers: Critical Insights to Engage Engineers in a New Decade (TREW Marketing and IEEE GlobalSpec).

Engineers value supplier/vendor websites, search engine results, and technical publications most as sources of content.

As you can see from the chart, 56 percent of respondents rated supplier and vendor websites as very valuable. Search engines and trade publication websites followed closely at 33 percent and 32 percent, respectively.

In terms of overall value, we see emails and enewsletters coming in the fourth spot, with high marks from respondents indicating they are either very or somewhat valuable. GenX engineers place high value on emails and enewsletters compared to their older and younger peers.

YouTube gained significantly in popularity, with thirty-two percent citing this channel as very valuable, up from twenty-six percent the previous year. As Millennials move into specifier and decision-making roles, and Gen Zers enter the workforce, expect this upwards trend to continue.

Looking at the least valuable channels is also helpful. Social media's low ranking has significant impact, as social has become part of a marketer's standard toolkit. Digging a bit deeper into social, the research found that engineers use social for networking, keeping up with news and trends, and finding job opportunities. The research also weighed in on the value engineers place on social platforms, found later in this chapter.

Another research study on B2B buyers had similar findings related to the value of content sources. In the B2B Content Marketing 2019: Benchmarks, Budgets, and Trends Report, the top five formats B2B marketers use to distribute content are email (93 percent), social media (92 percent), blogs (79 percent), in-person events (56 percent), and webinars (55 percent). When those same respondents were asked which of these formats were most effective, email was a standout winner at 74 percent, followed by blogs and social media at 45 percent and 40 percent, respectively.

Website Promotion

Start by scanning your site for locations to promote your content, particularly those pages most relevant to the content topic. For instance, a technical white paper might be promoted on a relevant industry page and product page. You can use white papers as a collection in a resource library or on a content hub or feature them on a relevant pillar page.

Another example is a new product web page, which would naturally live within the hierarchy of your website in a product family. But you might also promote your new product on relevant industry pages and as a product launch news item or blog post feature. This cross-linking between pages creates content relationships similar to those fostered by pillar pages, which helps both site visitors and search engines find related information across your website.

For new and meaty content pieces, consider creating a link or mini-ad for your content using a headline and imagery. The image might be an actual thumbnail of the cover or another illustrative image. A good tool for quick image creation is Canva. Your mini-ad should be clickable and link to the landing page.

Depending on your marketing automation platform's capabilities, you can create pop-up promotional boxes for your mini-ad. Be judicious with these pop-ups: The larger, more obnoxious versions may repel your engineer visitors, particularly if placed near subject matter unrelated to the pop-up. If you are utilizing a smart content strategy, create an ad that targets personas interested in the ad's subject matter and then place the ad on your website in an area with related content.

Calls to Action (CTAs)

Calls to action help guide visitors from one web page to the next through hyperlinked words, eye-catching buttons, or other images. They are often a bright or different color than the text on your site, and they explicitly describe what action the user should take (e.g. download, contact us, request a quote, etc.).

When you're brainstorming how to implement effective CTAs on your website, start by thinking through how your target persona interacts with your website. For example, a plant manager looking for a technical solution may visit your site to learn about the services you provide, the industries you serve, your company profile, and how you're different from your competitors.

The plant manager may then want to understand where and how you've implemented a similar solution before. By offering a case study as a CTA from your industry and service pages, you provide more information in context and lead buyers into the next stages of their journeys.

Graphic buttons are an effective way to direct users' eyes toward the next step or the actions you want them to take on your site when perusing a page. Bold and well-designed buttons that incorporate action-oriented verbiage are more likely to convert your users.

You can create unique graphic CTA buttons in tools like Canva that take users to lead-generating content. These images can be repurposed into your social media posts.

Examples of CTA buttons.

Social Media

Social media is a platform for sharing information, ideas, career interests, and other communication through virtual communities and networks. In short, social channels are a good place to share your information and gather feedback.

Feeling skeptical about investing in social media to reach your technical buyer? Let's examine the various outlets and consider how they fit with your target personas and overall content marketing strategy.

Choosing Social Outlets

As you begin to determine where to invest in owned social media, big social media platforms spring to mind first: YouTube, LinkedIn, Facebook, Instagram, and Twitter.

Beyond those, virtual communities and networks offer communication channels for specific audiences in industry verticals. Stack Overflow, for example, is touted as the "world's largest developer community," with over fifty million developer visits monthly. The Control System Integrators Association (CSIA) Exchange helps educate readers about system integration through Q&As and connects companies with

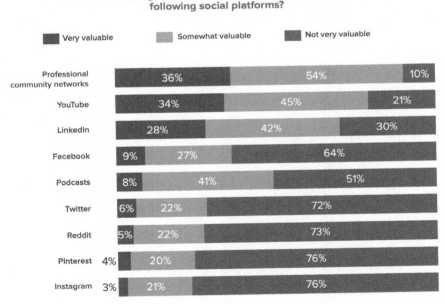

Data from 2020 Smart Marketing for Engineers: Critical Insight to Engage Engineers in a New Decade (TREW Marketing and IEEE GlobalSpec) shows that professional community networks, YouTube, and LinkedIn are seen as most valuable.

system integrators. IBM's application-centric communities feature both content discussions and blogs.

Younger engineers ranked YouTube first, whereas engineers aged 65+ strongly preferred professional community networks.

Podcasts were viewed as very or somewhat valuable at forty-nine percent combined, as opposed to Facebook coming in at thirty-six percent combined. A whopping seventy-two percent of engineers say that Twitter is not very valuable, and the same goes for Instagram at seventy-six percent not valuable.

With this data in mind, combined with your company's own social performance metrics, you may want to consider shifting some of your social marketing budget and sales social efforts away from lesser preferred and low-performing channels towards the popular and rising channels. Here is a breakdown of the top social channels and their roles within your content strategy.

LinkedIn

- **Purpose**: Professional networking
- **Priority**: High
- **Why**: B2B-oriented, targets very specific audience groups, SEO boost
- **Length of Post Allowed**: 600 characters for regular posts, 280 if dual-posting to Twitter
- **Recommended Length**: 190 characters, dual post with image (any longer is cut off with ellipses)

Twitter

- **Purpose**: Sharing and interacting via microposts
- **Priority**: Low
- **Function for B2B**: Boost SEO, interact during events
- **Length of Post**: Up to 280 characters
- **Recommended Length**: Fewer than 280 characters, short text with images are best

TREW Marketing
1,435 followers
1w • ℗

These 10 keys will strengthen the skills and knowledge you need to be a successful marketing manager in a technical, B2B company.
https://hubs.ly/H0nsBNI0

10 Keys to Success as a Technical Marketing Manager

trewmarketing.com

This dual post to LinkedIn and Twitter meets character limits.

YouTube

- **Purpose**: Video sharing
- **Priority**: High
- **Why**: Wholly owned subsidiary of Google, top global repository and search engine for video, second-largest search engine
- **Size of Upload**: Less than fifteen minutes for new accounts, less than twenty GB for verified accounts
- **Recommended Length**: Less than two minutes unless video is deeply technical, in which case it can run five to ten minutes

Introducing Storyboard 6.0 – Create big customer experiences for small embedded devices
117 views

Crank Software
Published on Jon 3, 2019

Crank Software's latest release Storyboard 6.0 is taking the next step forward in helping teams build products with great UIs for the world of embedded devices. Download the FREE Crank Storyboard Trial at ‣ www.cranksoftware.com/free-trial

Category   Howto & Style

YouTube is a perfect spot for hosting on-demand software demos.

Facebook and Instagram

- **Purpose**: Social networking

- **Priority**: Low

- **Function for B2B**: Share cultural aspects of company

- **Differences**:

- **Facebook** is more heavily used by GenX and older

- **Instagram** (owned by Facebook) is image-centric and more heavily used by millennials and younger

- **Length of Post**: Facebook—63,206 characters; Instagram—2,200 characters

- **Recommended Length**: 280 characters, similar to LinkedIn and Twitter

Use Facebook to communicate about your company culture.

Consider taking a practical multichannel approach. By using marketing tools such as Hootsuite or HubSpot, you can easily schedule posts across social channels. Then with your prioritized social channels, work to build a following, interact, and measure.

Creating Social Posts

To build and engage a social following, you need to post frequently with material suited for your target personas. Use thoughtful and technical content in all your social posts. Don't be fluffy! Fluff hurts your credibility and decreases your website's click-through rate. If you have hired your teenager to moonlight as your social media coordinator, you need to make sure your posts are consistent with the high-quality content you are producing elsewhere. Your posts should address your personas' pain points and concerns and match the tone you set for your brand.

Every post needs an image to grab your audience's attention. Visual content is forty times more likely to be shared socially than text only.

Use social media to continually promote your content. Your audience may not see your social post, so be sure to promote it again a few weeks later. Or, if you wrote in the past about a topic that develops some buzz later, promote that post in social media and point people back to your thoughts on the topic.

Include engaging images in your Twitter posts to improve click-through rates.

Speaking of sharing, how can you make it as easy as possible for your blog subscribers to interact with and pass along your high-quality content? Incorporate social sharing buttons your readers can use to forward your content via LinkedIn, Twitter, email, and other outlets.

Include your social media posts as part of your overarching content calendar you created in the planning phase. Your post frequency may range from daily to weekly and directly correlate with the pace at which you are creating new content, such as your blogging frequency.

During events, you may post as many as eight times a day using an event hashtag that attendees can easily find.

You can work more efficiently and gain deeper insights by using marketing tools such as HubSpot and Hootsuite. With these tools, you can write your social media posts when convenient and schedule them months in advance to post on multiple social platforms. You can also monitor others' posts on key topics and respond accordingly.

In addition to your company's social account, consider the power of your employees' social networks to extend your reach. As much as you might like to require every employee to post everything you publish, that is a bit of an overstep. Perhaps instead start simple: Share new content pieces with employees and suggest they "like" or post relevant information to their networks. If folks are receptive to this but not sure how to post, hold a mini training session on the basics of social media posting or record a short training video. If this is a key and regular strategy for your company, create company social media guidelines to help maintain consistency and avoid sticky situations. If you end up landing a big sale that originating from an employee's social post, share the success to encourage more company-wide posting.

Online Advertising

Driving traffic to your content through organic search is always best, but sometimes you need traffic and leads *now,* particularly if your sales team is idle and hungry. Search ranking improvements are a long game, and paid content placement (or online advertising) can be a great way to supplement your efforts.

With online advertising, you essentially pay a fee to get in front of a community that someone else has already gathered. The community organizer might be an industry online site (often with a print magazine or journal counterpart), a directory listing, a search engine, or a social media platform.

According to TREW's research and experience, the top places to promote technical content are LinkedIn, YouTube, and specific, relevant
industry online sites. You might be surprised that Google Advertising
did not make the top list. Our experience has shown us that (1) engineers are very aware and very wary of Google ads, and (2) the leads
produced by Google ads are routinely unqualified. Certainly there are
exceptions, and testing any ad on any platform is highly encouraged,
but perhaps start elsewhere if your budget is limited.

Create an ad for your content asset by following these steps:

1. Set Ad Goals and Target Audience

Do you want viewers to register for your upcoming webinar or read a
new case study? Are you trying to reach high-value personas and convert them to leads? Or, maybe you just want to raise awareness and send
new visitors to your website. The first step of any ad should be defining
that goal and the action an ad viewer should take. This helps you pinpoint the landing page you use and the audience you target.

You can run an ad to garner video views or increase blog post engagement, but it's more common to use ads to drum up leads or website
visits. Keep in mind that you'll likely be spending $3 or more per click,
so select a goal worthy of the investment. At TREW, we create ads for
high-value, gated content such as ebooks and webinars to generate new,
high-quality leads for our database.

Next, identify your target audience and define the qualities of that
audience. This process varies for each online platform, from no choices
to many choices.

Consider the typical attributes below, as defined by LinkedIn's Ad
Manager. Keep in mind that if you choose too many attributes, your list
may shrink your audience to the point that you can't produce results.
Consider these to be "ands" instead of "ors" in your selection process.

- **Location**: Required but also a common-sense choice. Where do
  you conduct business? Limit the ad to that geographic region.

- **Field of Study**: Your audience is likely made up of well-educated people in a very specific niche. Field of study can be a good way to hit this niche or a broader segment if there's a specific degree or program for it (e.g., aerospace engineering).

- **Company Industry**: Field of study might not be good enough when defining your audience if your target audience holds a generic engineering degree. Company industry can then help you narrow down to the specific vertical or function you focus on.

- **Degree and Job Function**: These two factors fine-tune your audience. Consider the job level, job function, and purchasing power of your intended audience. Are they current engineers or are they directors? Do they have advanced degrees? Add these factors in to target the specific group you need and avoid paying to reach the wrong people.

- **Note**: According to LinkedIn, a good rule of thumb is to keep the target audience size over 50,000 and always test to find the right range for your company.

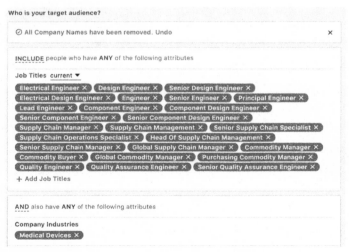

With LinkedIn you can be highly prescriptive when selecting who will view your ad

2. Build Your Landing Page and Post-Submission Actions

If your ad goal is to capture leads, chances are that when clicked, your ad takes someone to a landing page. You're paying to get people to this page, so put great care into its wording, imagery, form fields, and form length to ensure that it supports your goal and fits your persona.

If you are asking the visitor to complete a form to receive a piece of content, consider additional communication touchpoints and calls to action once the visitor submits the form. For example, the visitor may complete a form for a white paper. After delivering that content asset, send an email as part of a multitouch email workflow that provides related content items, such as case studies or demos, designed to push prospects along their buyer's journey. You will learn more about workflows later in this chapter.

3. Create Ad Elements

You know your goal and target audience, and you have a specific landing page to promote. Now, you can write the ad copy, select an image (if included), and ready the landing page link.

Character limits and image dimensions vary by ad type and publisher. Make sure you research the best practices for that ad type before crafting imagery and content. For example, some ad formats such as Facebook limit the amount of text you can include in an ad graphic.

If possible, develop several versions of the ad and obtain team input on them. This ensures that you have a backup if you need to change out an underperforming ad.

Don't forget to prepare your landing page link at this point. To accurately attribute website traffic and conversions to a specific ad and campaign, add UTM codes using your marketing automation tool or Google's URL builder.

4. Set Up and Launch Your Ads

We typically run two versions of an ad with either a different image or text to A/B test an element. Make sure your budget can support running more than one ad and that you're prepared to closely monitor and act on performance.

5. Evaluate and Make Changes

Your ad(s) may be live, but you're far from done. Check the ad performance at least weekly, monitoring the cost per click, overall clicks, click-through rate, and conversions/leads. Some platforms such as LinkedIn provide forecasted results when you set up the ad, and you can compare your results to past performance or ad benchmarks.

Other metrics to keep an eye on are form conversions, conversion rate, number of new leads, new visitors from the ads, and the engagement length of the ad visitors versus the average engagement length. Reviewing all these metrics ensures that you stay on track for your goal and can course correct if it looks like something isn't working.

Industry Presentations

According to research conducted by TREW Marketing and IEEE Global-Spec, eighty-two percent of engineers rate industry events as a very or somewhat valuable way to research technical purchase decisions.

Your company can participate in an event in a wide range of ways, from the simple "walking the show" to a full exhibit and sponsorship. Among all the options, the one with the lowest cost per lead and highest ROI is to deliver a presentation at a highly relevant technical conference. By presenting, your spokesperson and company are positioned as experts and thought leaders. You engage a highly qualified audience, retain the ability to control your message, and—if you do it correctly—capture leads.

During a presentation, your spokesperson becomes the voice of your company and makes a significant impact on how your company and solutions are perceived. Be thoughtful when selecting this person! It can be a difficult balancing act, particularly when presenting on technical topics. The person most technically astute about the topic may be the least comfortable and experienced telling that story to an external audience, whereas the opposite may apply to your most talented company orator.

To be an effective technical spokesperson, you need to:

1. Match the Level of Technical Detail with Your Audience Profile

Though your wealth of knowledge is a strength, you must communicate it effectively to have an impact. Your audience may have different levels of technical acumen, so you need to adjust the presentation accordingly.

2. Tailor Messaging to the Audience

Depending on the diversity of audience needs, consider spending more time providing context and examples related to a product or solution. Why is this spec or feature important? What are the different ways this can be used or implemented? Where has this been implemented? Why is your way better? Don't forget to tailor this information to the audience (e.g., lead with an example relevant to the industry conference).

3. Anticipate Questions

You'll likely be asked about competitors, specifications, and alternatives. Be prepared! Also, politely steer clear of off-topic questions by suggesting an offline discussion.

4. Capture Attention and Build Rapport

Effective presenters draw in the audience with tactics that include the following:

- Start with a story and striking image
- Get to a product demo quickly; err toward more demo and discussion and less PowerPoint
- Use case studies or real-world examples to illustrate your points versus just stating them
- Demonstrate your own passion for the subject
- Involve the audience by asking questions about their experience or opinions on the topic; you could even conduct a pre-event poll if you know who will be attending and use the results to drive home your key points

5. Make Adjustments

You may believe that your story is fascinating, but the audience may not be that interested. At this point, your challenge is to adjust accordingly. Great spokespeople don't just run through their presentations. They are always aware of the audience's level of engagement. Spend more time on subjects that engage the group and sacrifice other areas that don't seem to be hitting home.

6. Speak to the Industry

To build trust with your audience members, you need to understand the challenges they face and speak to them beyond the specific desire to promote your company's solutions. Your spokesperson should both know and have opinions about the trends in the industry.

7. Use Real-World Examples

One of the best ways to validate your main message is by providing real-world examples. These can be quick mentions or the meat of the presentation. The examples should be relevant to the audience and the focus of the event as a whole. You can source them from your own customers, big companies in the industry, and other vendors, or you can use unnamed generic examples.

8. Close with a Call to Action

How would you like to further engage with the audience? Typical tactics include offering the presentation slides and other content resources through a landing page specific to the event. You can use a Bitly URL to provide a super short and memorable address for this or simply your URL plus the event name. Ask attendees to complete a short form in exchange for the content resources.

Email Marketing and Database Management

Email remains the value-to-results leader for engaging with the contacts in your database. A whopping eight-three percent of engineers surveyed found email and enewsletters to be highly or somewhat valuable when seeking information on engineering technologies, trends, and products. Given the important role of email in your content marketing strategy, this section dives into several aspects of this promotional channel: database management, enewsletters, email campaigns, and email nurturing workflows.

Email marketing must be handled with the utmost care and respect. You've worked your tail off creating and serving up compelling content on your website, and in exchange your technical prospects have entrusted you with their contact information. Don't blow it now!

You (and your sales team) should live by the following tenets:

- I shall protect the confidentiality of my contacts' information
- I will not spam my contacts with either overcommunication or irrelevant communication
- I shall use an email platform with features that ensure that I employ best practices when emailing my database (e.g., Hub-Spot, ConstantContact, MailChimp, etc.)
- I will offer a way to unsubscribe and take action if a contact requests it, in accordance with the privacy laws of my region

Database Management

Email marketing programs are only as good as the data in your CRM. Before you ramp up on email, be sure you have a clean database. The opposite, a dirty database, is usually caused by neglect (e.g., scads of old contacts who left their jobs a decade ago) and by zealous entry (e.g., uploads of a bulk attendee list you got your hands on from an event where you exhibited). Heed my warning: If you skip this step, you may be shut down by your email platform or blacklisted by your internet service provider due to a low deliverability rate!

You can choose from several options to clean your CRM. The easiest, provided you have a decent CRM tool in place, is to create an automated workflow. This workflow is programmed to look for and remove old and bad contacts as indicated by a hard bounce (e.g., invalid email address). If you don't have an automation tool, or your bounce rate is high despite your workflow, use an email service to clean up your email addresses. You should also address duplicate contacts on a regular basis. Check out your Sender Score at sendorscore.com to see what your email sender reputation is.

While you're focused on database management, document your strategy. Think through rules defining how frequently you email contacts and how you protect their data. Then address those through people, processes, and technology. Two elements to include are permissions and segmentation.

Permissions

Even if your business doesn't extend beyond the United States, consider adopting permission-based email marketing. With this approach, you see a higher level of engagement, gain better insight into your content performance, and save yourself from exhaustion over efforts with low-potential leads. The easiest way to do this is to offer subscriptions to your enewsletter, blog, or other company emails via a subscription page. Promote these subscriptions throughout your website. If you're already sending emails to lists of people who haven't explicitly opted in, send a "re-permissioning" email asking them to confirm their subscriptions. Don't forget to include unsubscribe as an option on every email, and immediately unsubscribe readers when they direct you to do so.

Now that your CRM is clean and ready for email action, let's get moving on email marketing.

Enewsletters

Enewsletters are an effective way to stay in touch with your prospects and customers, establish thought leadership, and keep your brand top of mind during a long sales cycle. Due to the aggregated nature of their content, enewsletters are typically planned for a monthly or quarterly send cadence. This helps prevent the communication fatigue generated when organizations send emails on a whim to promote something seemingly random to prospects and customers (recipients often equate these communications to spamming). Excessive emails drive contacts to unsubscribe. As hard as you've worked to collect new contacts, you need to be thoughtful and protective of how you communicate with them.

For more than a decade, enewsletters have been a popular information source for engineers. Engineers subscribe to an average of three to five enewsletters at any given time. Did your enewsletter make the cut?

Done right, your enewsletter should be easy to publish. It promotes the content you've already created instead of requiring you to create new content.

To design and publish a high-performing enewsletter, keep in mind the following:

1. Frequency

Choose a frequency that allows time for you to create new content and keeps you top of mind with your readers. Quarterly is a good starting point if you are new to content marketing; monthly is better if you are a regular content producer. Weekly is a bit too frequent for most companies to handle.

2. Design

Think of your enewsletter as prime real estate for your company and brand. Your design should be consistent from issue to issue and offer staying power for many issues to come. The key to good design is usability; make your enewsletter easy to open, skim, and find articles and links in that are compelling. Most popular email platforms provide email templates that follow usability standards and can be easily customized to your brand standards. These design templates should render correctly no matter which platform or device viewers are using.

3. Subject Line

Be creative and succinct. Test different types of headlines (see our discussion of A/B testing below), and, once you have identified a preferred method, be consistent. Keep in mind that email clients often display part of your preheader as a preview snippet. Ensure that this small line of text is a well-crafted message because it may make the difference between an open and a delete.

Of engineers surveyed, 47 percent subscribe to three or more enewsletters.

4. Content

Develop content that is 90 percent helpful and 10 percent promotional. It's tempting to write enewsletter content about sales-driven topics such as new promotions, but focus instead on educational content that helps readers do their jobs better. Keep it short and avoid jargon, unnecessary details, and fluff. Include a brief summary of an article or a content resource, an image, and a prominent link to read more.

A mix of content types including the following works best:

• Industry trend infographics
• Tutorial or "tips and tricks" videos
• Case studies
• "Top X" list
• Post-event wrap-up

A great way to assess your enewsletter content and design is through A/B testing. First, pinpoint one thing you want to learn from the test. For example, maybe you're wondering if you'd get a better open rate by featuring only one article in the subject line instead of multiple articles. Then split your distribution list in half and send one group the single-topic subject line and the other group the multiple-topic subject line. The group with the best open rate wins. The next time you send your enewsletter, use what you learned and pick another topic to analyze.

A Note on Privacy

Many countries have laws that regulate the use of citizens' data and protect their citizens' privacy. Each law is different in scope and severity and may be enforced by different groups, depending on the country. Acquaint yourself with the various laws and ensure that you are compliant. The top laws for U.S. companies to be aware of in 2020 include the General Data Protection Regulation (GDPR), Controlling the Assault of Non-Solicited Pornography and Marketing Act of 2003 (CAN-SPAM), and California Consumer Privacy Act (CCPA).

Online privacy is taken very seriously by many states and countries, with strict penalties for noncompliance of privacy laws. Follow these best practices:

- Contact only the people who have expressly opted-in to messages from your company.
- Allow contacts to enroll in subscription types and send only the types of information they request.
- If you're unsure of a contact list's origin or age, don't use it! The consequences could be severe.
- Don't buy or sell contact data.
- Ensure that your cookie policies are up to date, include a link to the full privacy policy, and offer options to accept or decline the policy.
- Give contacts a way to unsubscribe or request full deletion of their information.
- Stay up to date on privacy regulations and update your company's processes as needed.

Many email tools incorporate an A/B testing feature to automatically divide your list, test the versions, and send the winning version to the remainder of the list. Take advantage of this feature to quickly gain insight and act on it.

Once you've designed your enewsletter and developed a clear vision for succinct, compelling content, you need to build your readership. Though it's tempting to email every contact in your database and more, you can adopt a smarter approach to generate more loyalty and better results. Focus on only your most relevant leads: those who have contacted you in the last twelve to twenty-four months. Older leads are less likely to remember you or be interested in and open your enewsletter. In addition, older leads commonly include invalid or outdated email addresses, and your enewsletter will bounce back when you send it to them.

Email Campaigns

Email "blasts" are so 1990s (or they should be). Effective email campaigns start with a specific topic and audience in mind. The topic should be something important and time-sensitive, such as a new product or upcoming event. Otherwise, you should hold your content for your enewsletter. The audience should not be everyone in your CRM (no "blasting!") but rather a segment of your database who will find the topic relevant. By segmenting and personalizing your email content, you can ensure your email a better chance of resonating with the intended audience (see chapter 10 for performance metrics). By segmenting, you also greatly lower the risk of losing contacts who don't find the information relevant and choose to opt out of communications from your company.

Don't panic if this is all new to you. Your segmentation doesn't necessarily need to be complex to achieve a bump in results. That being said, without the data in place in your CRM, you are dead in the water.

Think through the major ways you would like to segment (e.g., persona, industry, life-cycle stage, etc.) and run reports in your CRM to make sure that data is populated for most of your database. If you have holes, you can plug these through automation as well. For example, your persona may be closely tied to job title. Your workflow could map job titles to the persona and populate this field.

Setting Up an Email Campaign

Start by identifying the subject and goal of the email campaign. For example, you are hosting a live seminar, "Nine Security Risks with Autonomous Vehicle Sensors," and your goal is to secure 150 registrants and 75 live-event attendees.

You likely already thought about your target audience when you created the webinar content, so now you need to think about which database fields you can use to identify and email that audience. You are considering industry (automotive) and job title (design engineer) as criteria. To meet your goal, you need around ten times your target number of relevant contacts to email. Don't have that many names? Consider (a) co-marketing with a partner to leverage both of your databases for a larger pool or (b) revising your goal to a more reasonable target.

Next, consider how many touches are needed to entice someone to register. For an event-related email, two to three email touches are typical to produce results. You need to measure each email touch's impact to see which yielded the most registrants and whether the third touch was worth the extra outreach. Don't forget that if you are sending an enewsletter during this timeframe, you can promote the event through that vehicle and skip one of your direct emails.

Also, think through what happens after someone registers. You need to send them a thank you email, instructions for logging in, and a reminder the day before or the day of the event. It's best to automate all this through your marketing automation or webinar technology platform. (See more on automated email workflows below.)

Now that you have your goals, audience, and emails mapped out, you need to write, design, and send. The best practices for this are similar to those covered in the enewsletter section:

- Short, compelling subject line (if event-related, consider including the date)
- Thoughtful pre-header snippet
- Succinct content with a visual, two to four short paragraphs, and possibly a bulleted list
- Links to a deeper information dive and one primary call to action for readers to take their next step
- Clean, simple design to emphasize your content and call to action; use templates provided by your email technology platform provider for easy setup

Email Nurturing

Now let's switch gears to email nurturing. As opposed to enewsletters, which reach a broad audience of subscribers or perhaps even your entire database, and unlike email campaigns, which are segmented but still reach a relatively large audience, email nurturing is highly targeted.

Email nurturing is a tactic aimed at helping prospects dig deeper into their research on your company and the solutions you offer. You achieve this by serving up content in the context of an action the prospect has recently taken. The always-on, automated aspects of email nurturing help your company qualify leads for sales in an efficient, low-cost manner, particularly when compared with the cost of an inside sales qualifier. The following steps can help you set up an automated email nurture.

First, identify your audience, goals, and triggers. You should base your nurture on personas who have taken a certain action or a set of actions that indicate they are ready to enter the next phase of the buyer's journey. Your goal might be to entice a prospect to meet sales, fill out a product configurator, or sign up for a demo, to name a few. You may also want to exclude certain contacts, such as customers or leads sales has disqualified.

Here is an example of this step:

- **Persona Target**: Design Engineer Dan
- **Goal**: Request for a demo board
- **Actions Taken Prior to Workflow**: Downloaded a particular white paper or watched a recorded webinar on a similar subject
- **Exclusions**: Customers, lead status of unqualified

Next, brainstorm later-stage content assets that are related to the actions that the prospect has already taken. These might include a short video, product spec page, and case study. It is often helpful to pull in product, service delivery, and sales resources to gain varied perspectives on the content that will best appeal to your target audience. All these content pieces help educate and lead the conversation toward the goal.

With the content in mind, plan your workflow. Determine the number of emails to send, the timeframe between each email, and the actions a lead can take to opt out of the workflow, such as a content download or life-cycle stage to an opportunity. If you are just starting out with email nurturing, begin with a workflow of three to five emails in a three- to seven-day frequency. Once you have the hang of this tactic, you can experiment with branching logic and more emails over a longer period of time.

Using your workflow framework, assign a content topic and call to action to each email. Keep your emails concise and present one clear next step. The call to action might be a piece of content in the first one to two emails and then a more sales-oriented call to action in the last set of emails. (Tip: Use a calendar tool so leads can schedule time with an expert directly from the email.)

The final steps are to build the nurture into your tool, test it, and launch. Once it has run fully for a short period of time, measure and tweak its performance. Consider swapping a subject line, changing a call to action, testing timing, or replacing low-performing emails altogether. Iteration is key with this tactic.

Remember, email nurtures should be targeted to the needs of the people receiving it and genuinely helpful in their stage of the buyer's journey.

Subscriptions

Subscriptions are an effective way for the contacts in your database to choose what and when they want to hear from you. They not only receive a service from you but also provide you with feedback. Subscriptions are a good sign that your material is well received by your target personas because you know they want to hear more from you. This tactic also helps with all those privacy laws we discussed earlier. Because readers opt-in to a subscription, they are granting you permission to send them communication.

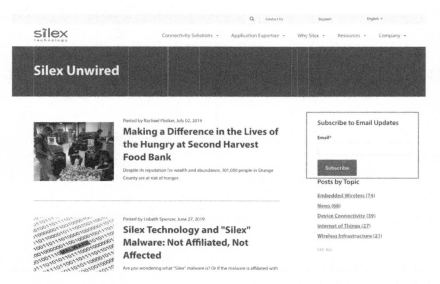

Silex Technology offers a simple, one-field subscription form in key areas of its website.

Consider offering subscriptions for several different categories of content, such as your blog, enewsletter, company or product news, and event information. To earn subscribers, promote subscription options in different areas of your website, particularly the footer. Include an option on your blog page above the fold so that it's easily noticeable. In addition, consider sending an email to your contacts encouraging them to subscribe and share periodically via social media.

Once readers click on the subscription link, they should be directed to a landing page with a form that explains the different subscription options, purpose of each, topics they cover, benefits of subscribing, and frequency of delivery. By completing the form, subscribers receive this type of content automatically (you set up a marketing automation workflow for this).

Lead nurturing workflows begin with a prospect's action and are programmed to send emails in a time-based duration.

Section Four
Sales Enablement

Chapter 9
CREATE SALES CONTENT THAT CONVERTS

Remember the days when salespeople held all the cards? They were the keepers of technical information, the guards of pricing, and the purchasers of nice dinners.

Today, industry research, including findings from TREW surveys of engineers globally, shows that the technical buyers those salespeople are trying to reach aren't necessarily looking for social activities. Engineers are conducting research, evaluating vendors online, and delaying their engagement with sales until they are well down the path of the buying process. This shift presents an enormous challenge to companies still using the old-school sales gatekeeper approach.

In thinking about the entire buying process for significant purchases you make for work, from early research to the final purchase decision, what percentage of the process happens online before you finally choose to speak to someone at the company?

▥ Over 70%   ▪ 50% to 70%   ▪ Under 50%

25%   48%   26%

More than 50 percent of the buyer's journey happens before buyers engage with sales. 2020 Smart Marketing for Engineers: Critical Insights to Engage Engineers in a New Decade (TREW Marketing and IEEE GlobalSpec).

Today, successful salespeople serve as educators and advisers. From helping engineers understand which products are the best fit for their

applications to proving that your company is the best fit for their needs to
walking a prospect through software
licensing options to simply serving as
your brand personified, salespeople are
critical and their time is valuable.

Today, successful
salespeople serve
as educators and
advisers.

In chapter 3, you learned about the
importance of including key salespeople
in content planning. Sales and market-
ing work together to map out one seamless experience for the prospect
and to deliver value and build trust through content at each touchpoint
in the buyer's journey.

Often marketing teams make the mistake of ending their content
planning at the lead-capture or lead-nurture step. They forget that once
the handoff to sales occurs, sales advisers need content to support their
efforts. This content usually includes a mixture of assets that marketing
can create, such as case studies and technical specification web pages,
along with new types of assets that support the sales process, such as
email scripts and presentation slides.

Conduct a Sales Content Assessment

Start your planning process by identifying where you are today.
You can evaluate every content asset and its potential for sales use or
examine the pieces your sales organization already relies on to engage
prospects and customers. If you are not sure where to start, keep your
study open-ended and spend time learning what your sales team uses.
Whatever method you choose, carve a path to uncover surprises.

For example, you might start with a brief survey of the members
of your sales force to learn which content pieces they find most helpful when prospecting and managing an opportunity. You can give them
examples (e.g. case studies, ROI calculators, etc.) or keep it completely
open-ended.

Supplement this survey with data on how your content is performing (if you have this data, it is typically housed in your marketing automation or content management platform). Pay particular attention to the statistics on the role of content in influencing a sale. Learn more on this in chapter 10.

You also want to explore the points in the sales process where marketing-generated content can help. Here are some examples:

Troubleshooting Sales with Marketing Efforts

Issue	How Marketing Can Help
Low Connect Rate With Prospects	Email Templates and Scripts
Losing Out to Competitors	Revamp Value Proposition
Struggling to Bridge from Technical Specifier to Executive Decision Maker	Business Impact Case Study
Skeptical Buyer, Lack of Credibility	Case Studies
Low Linkedin Following/ Interactions	Educational Content for Social Sharing, Sponsored Content
Can't Find Content	Central, Searchable Repository
Not Enough Bandwidth to Contact Leads	Prequalification Through Lead Scoring
Opportunities Fizzling Out at High Rates	Evaluate Prospect Rating Criteria Evaluation
Penetrating New Accounts	Targeted, Account-Specific Content

Catalog and audit all sales content assets, making note of the outdated, most used, and least used items. Also include how easy or difficult it was to find each item.

By the end of your sales content assessment, you will have a comprehensive view of which content assets sales and your personas most love and a list of ideas for new content to serve their needs in the future.

Sales Enablement Content

We've walked through the many purposes of marketing content: to attract interest and introduce your company to a prospect, position your brand, and build enough trust that your prospects will share their valuable contact information with you. Research shows that most engineers have three to four interactions with a company before wanting to connect with a salesperson. Your prospects consume a substantial amount of content before their first sales conversation!

The pressure is now on the salesperson to meet prospects where they are in their buyer's journeys. They need to have relevant, impactful conversations that add value and build trust. To do this, sales content should use personalization and context to communicate value and urgency and overcome objections.

Top Sales Enablement Content

Every company has some sales content pieces that have withstood the test of time as most helpful for its sales team. These often include:

- PowerPoint presentations
- Detailed product specs and CAD drawings
- Product demo videos
- Competitive research
- Comparison tables
- Knowledge-base articles or FAQs
- In-depth case studies

- Return on investment (ROI) and total cost of ownership (TCO) calculators
- Internal proof-of-concept documentation

What makes these particular content assets so popular?

When technical buyers engage a salesperson, their typical first need is to identify a solution that meets their technical specifications and is both proven in the industry and able to provide more value than other options. If their applications are innovative, more risk might be necessary to meet their specifications through an unproven technology or product.

Go-to content at this stage is frequently a PowerPoint presentation deck or whiteboarding script that contains a mixture of features, benefits, and case studies. Salespeople almost always customize this deck for their customers. By uncovering typical customizations (industry, application, etc.), you can offer a library of slides from which sales mixes and

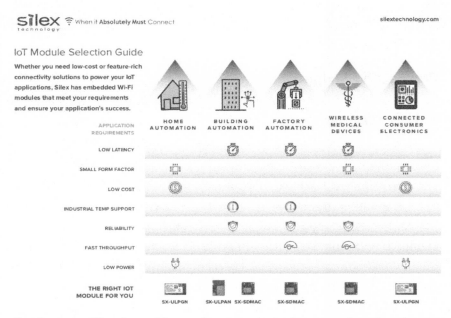

Product specification tables and comparison charts are handy reference tools for your sales team and prospects.

matches for the right personalized approach. Learn more about creating a compelling presentation deck in chapter 5.

Product specification tables and comparison charts are handy reference tools for your sales team and prospects.

As buyers short-list your solution, they still may need to choose from a variety of options that meet their needs. The next step for them is determining which solution provides the most value. This budget-related evaluation often involves comparing the price, return on investment (ROI), and total cost of ownership (TCO) for each option. Speed, support, and brand strength are also key considerations at this stage. The group may expand at this point to include a buying team, with different roles at the table (e.g., procurement, executive, etc.). Technical specifications then give way to business-oriented messaging and proof points. Be sure your library of go-to sales content includes resources for this stage.

Once you've created and honed the top sales enablement content assets, continue your partnership with sales to work on a few less considered and emerging areas: prospecting scripts, proposals, personalized video, and chat.

Prospecting Scripts

Who are the best writers in the company? Who is most in touch with every message that has been delivered to the prospect up until the point of handoff to sales? Marketing! Since marketing has been involved in all communications up to this point, it makes sense to involve marketing in writing sales emails and phone scripts as well. This is often an overlooked area, however, it is one of the biggest ways companies can improve conversion rates and gain sales efficiency. When coaching his clients, David Finkel, coauthor of *Build a Business, Not a Job,* increased their conversion rates by over 20 percent just by introducing better trust messaging and credibility enhancers.

Prospecting scripts are intended to efficiently guide outreach, but they do not stand alone. Your sales team uses data from the CRM to profile prospects and review their interactions with your company to date. They also do some digging on the prospects' company websites, LinkedIn profiles, and other company resources to prepare. Sales has a tried-and-true set of questions and speaking points to move the opportunity forward. All this being said, having strong prospecting outreach scripts helps sales efficiently and quickly make that initial connection.

Start with understanding the prospect outreach cadence sales uses today for a particular lead type. Identify the various scripts and templates used (if used at all) and identify areas where marketing could help strengthen sales outreach areas.

For example, a typical sales outreach cadence may follow this process:

By understanding the cadence used in sales prospecting, marketing can help to address conversion bottlenecks through sales enablement content.

Study the success metrics on connect rates within the cadence to determine where your company's strengths and gaps are today. These include email open rates and phone call connect rates. You may find that some of your salespeople are hitting home runs based on their scripts while others are not. Perhaps the more successful script becomes the default script for all. Conversely, you may find large inconsistencies in messaging, poor grammar, or other major issues that indicate a standardization initiative may help improve your connect rates.

You may be able to use your CRM or sales software platform to automate an email sales series for high-volume prospecting similar to marketing automation workflows. This software feature creates opportunities for sales to work more efficiently and for marketing to help keep messaging consistent as contacts flow into the sales pipeline.

Sales can use templated emails targeted to each persona type to address common sales outreach scenarios. They can use stand-alone emails or a series of emails that is often automated. This series is known as a sequence in some sales automation tools.

These tips can help you create sales scripts that convert:

- Be consistent with your corporate tone and voice. See chapter 1 for a reminder about this.

- Be authentic and helpful. Engineers are instantly turned away by cheesy or pressure-filled prose.

- Lead with benefits. Why should these prospects meet with your company? What will they get out of that meeting?

- Offer a relevant resource. If this lead originally generated from a hardware-in-the-loop webinar, offer another content resource related to that topic. It is a great way to give more value, test for lead quality, and endear prospects to the idea of a meeting with sales.

- Position the salesperson as a technical expert who's here to help.

- Make it personal! This is your opportunity to make the switch from one-to-many communication to one-to-one communication. Follow an 80 percent/20 percent rule where at least 20 percent of the script is personalized.

- Personalize efficiently with tokens. <Name> <Company> and <Company Description> are great ways to make your email feel personal without heavy lifting.
- Use a calendar tool. Make it easy for the prospect to schedule time with the salesperson through a calendar link. HubSpot and Calendly are both excellent tools with Gmail and Outlook plug-ins for this purpose.
- Consider offering content further along in the buyer's journey as calls to action to boost open and conversion rates.

Once you have drafted your scripts, review them with your sales and marketing alignment group, iterate on them, and finalize them. Have salespeople try out the new emails for a week and give you initial feed-back. Then step back for a good three to four weeks (at a minimum, wait the length of a full prospecting cycle) and measure results. Revisit connect rate metrics and see where you've moved the needle. Make modifications on a periodic basis as housekeeping or when you have a fantastic new content offering that works well in one of your scripts.

Proposal Development

When your prospect personally asks for a proposal, or your company chooses to respond to a request for proposal (RFP), this is a golden moment when strong content can make the difference between win-ning the sale and seeing all your hard work get tossed into the trash bin. If crafted with care, proposals can strengthen your company brand, forge alignment with your prospect, win over decision makers, and beat the competition.

Though proposals should always be customized by the person who is closest to the opportunity, there is a significant opportunity for mar-keting (as the best branders and writers in the company) to create a library of proposal templates and options for various proposal sections based on audience persona and solution type. Sales can pull from this template library, helping them to move further and faster in developing their custom proposal.

Let's walk through the typical proposal elements and best practices for constructing your proposal templates:

1. Proposal Cover

As the very first page of your proposal, the cover sets the tone for the document. It should have a memorable, professional design that aligns with your company brand standards and the types of solutions you offer. Be sure to include key information such as the proposal name, any necessary reference numbers, the client's name and logo, your company name and logo, and the submission date.

2. Executive Summary

Also known as an overview statement, the executive summary contains three to four paragraphs outlining key information included in the proposal. The summary should include the client's problem or need and a compelling synopsis of your company's solution. The purpose of this section is to demonstrate your knowledge of the customer's needs and why your solution is the best. Focus on benefits rather than features or specs.

3. Scope of Work

Also known as the approach, this meaty section includes a detailed description of your solution to the customer's problem or opportunity. It also ensures that you and your potential customer are aligned on deliverables. Your scope of work should clearly list the deliverables the client expects to receive. Make this section easier to read by using bullets or numbered or lettered lists. Include a timeline or create a new section with that information immediately following. The timeline may be high level, such as estimated time to completion, or detailed with a list of specific milestones or deliverables by dates.

4. Budget

The all-important "What does all this cost?" page might be the first page read because some potential customers skip straight there and then circle back to the rest of your proposal. Whether you have a fixed or hourly structure, make sure your budget items are easy to understand and that they clearly map back to the scope of work. Accuracy is key; triple check your calculations to be sure you are not undercharging or overcharging. A mistake here can have very large ramifications for your company's profitability! High-level payment terms are usually included in this section.

5. About Us

Also known as qualifications, this section is intentionally near the end of your proposal. Why? The client is most concerned with the solution and pricing proposed, and in your thoughtful approach to sections one through four, you have demonstrated your experience and gained your prospect's trust. This section should introduce who you are as a company, what services or products you offer (beyond those in the proposal), and how you are different. Pull from your corporate messaging to make this section consistent in branding. Think of this section as a way to strengthen your prospect's confidence in you as the chosen vendor, whether that be by including company values, case studies, or samples of work. An overview of the team members directly associated with the delivery of the proposed solution is often included in this section.

6. Terms, Conditions, and Signature

Ease the transition from proposal to contract by including contract language from the start; if this feels appropriate for your prospects, consider embedding tokens for client name and client contact within this section to personalize what is otherwise pretty standard text.

Now that you have a good grasp on the elements included in a proposal, you are ready to start constructing your library. Before you take this step, consider your development platform. In chapter 8, you learned how software can help you work smarter, and proposal construction is no exception. Numerous platforms, including PandaDoc and Proposify, help you create elegant proposal designs with a variety of drag-and-drop templates representing your products and services that are most frequently quoted. These tools often include features such as pricing tables, commenting, signature pages, and even analytics to measure opens, view time, and success rate.

Follow these tips to create a proposal that converts:

- **Design**: Design your proposal to be both memorable and easy to read; avoid cheesy stock photos, low-resolution images, or too many fonts and colors.

- **Language**: Use approachable language with a tone and voice that is authentic to your company culture. Avoid jargon and acronyms that may not be clear to some audience groups.

- **Personalization**: Use personalization tokens such as <Company Name> to customize efficiently. Demonstrate knowledge of your client's needs and describe how your solution can help. Show that you have been listening.

- **Clarity**: Perform a gut check for clarity. Is there a direct connection between your prospect's problem and your proposed solution? Does your scope of work leave any ambiguity about deliverables? Are your pricing and payment terms easy to understand?

- **Differentiation**: Ask, "Why?" Be sure your proposal answers why questions such as, "Why this solution?," "Why your company over a competitor?," and "Why now?" Your proposal should not just state the facts but also position your solution as the best choice.

Emerging B2B Sales Enablement Trends: Video and Chat

Video and chat provide opportunities to strengthen sales enablement, though you should use them strategically and thoughtfully to avoid distracting or deterring prospects.

Video

Video is an interesting and inexpensive method for salespeople to personalize their messages in a memorable way, particularly for companies conducting some or all of their sales processes by phone or online. It can also have a profound effect on your open rate. One study found a five-fold increase in email open rate and eight-fold increase in click-through rate for companies that incorporated videos into their sales processes.

Use videos for prospect outreach, a pre-meeting backgrounder, a quick demo, a follow-up, a thank you, and a reminder about signing that proposal, just to name a few. According to Wyzowl's 5th Annual State of Video Marketing survey, the most popular videos for sales conversations are demos and explainers (e.g., explaining a concept).

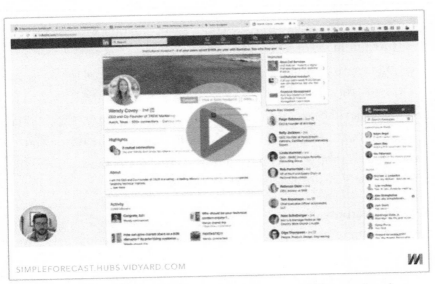

SIMPLEFORECAST.HUBS.VIDYARD.COM

Short, customized sales videos are memorable and humanize the salesperson.

Why is video a smart tactic? For your prospect, this is an interesting and fun way to hear your message. It humanizes the salesperson, which makes it more difficult to hit that delete button. Also, video is memorable. How many times have you received this type of message, if ever?

Here's the catch: It can be difficult to inspire sales to adopt a new way of doing things. Reduce friction by looking for video software platforms that launch quickly and are super easy to use; this shouldn't be more time-consuming than typing an email. You also may want to consider a three-month pilot with one adventurous salesperson, measure the results of that effort, and use the data to win over the rest of the team.

Also use this pilot to test which personas are most receptive to the video format. With most platforms, you can measure performance such as opens and duration watched. You may find this format to be popular with some personas and a turnoff for others.

Vidyard, Biteable, and Wistia are popular technology platforms to consider for your pilot project.

Follow these tips to create impactful sales videos:

- Keep your length to thirty seconds or less for quick messages and three minutes or less for product or solution content.
- Make sure your lighting and sound are adequate and the environment around you looks professional.
- Consider the use of props and ways to personalize, such as the whiteboard with the prospect's name shown in the image above.
- Create a short script for each prospecting stage; these scripts will be lightly customized and reused often.

Chat and Chatbots

Chat in the content marketing world refers to conversations held over the internet with your prospects or customers. Chat provides a way to help your prospects as they navigate your site by offering an experience that is way more personal than self-serve surfing. Chats help your marketing team by generating leads, your sales team by qualifying interests and securing that first valuable meeting, and your support team by fielding routine questions.

These are the dialogue boxes that pop up on a website and invite the visitor to converse with the company immediately. Some chats are live, meaning an actual person (typically a support or inside salesperson, based on the context of the page) responds. Other chats are conducted through a chatbot.

Early chatbots operated through multiple choice

AVP uses chat to engage prospects on its Aviary product page. See this chatbot in action at aviaryplatform.com.

scripts and workflows, but the newer versions use artificial intelligence (AI) software. AI bots are still evolving, and most B2B brands use scripted bots to ensure a predictable brand experience. Typical B2B interactions with chatbots focus on customer support, marketing, and sales.

There are many bullish predictions about future chatbot adoption. Business Insider experts predict that by 2020, 80 percent of enterprises will use chatbots. A survey conducted by Spiceworks showed that 40 percent of large companies employing more than 500 people plan to implement one or more intelligent assistant or AI-based chat robots over corporate mobile devices in 2019. And according to the Comm100 website, millennials, who are increasingly gaining the predominant purchasing power, consider instant messaging a preferred support channel.

That all sounds great, but the question on your mind is likely: "If I build it, will my engineer prospect come?"

The answer is a mixed one. Behavioral data shows that engineers place greater value on privacy than the average B2B buyer and do not give up information easily. The 2020 Smart Marketing for Engineers research report shows chatbots rank low on an engineer's list of information sources. That being said, adoption of chat and chatbots is high in consumer markets such as banking and retail, and typically this trains behavior that we then see on the B2B side. For now, the takeaway is to be cautious about investing in this type of platform. If you do, lean into personalization and steer away from an aggressive or generic approach that would repel the technical buyer.

How to Set Up a Chatbot

If you are ready to experiment with your first chatbot, follow these key steps to getting started.

1. Set Goals

What do you hope to achieve by adopting a chatbot? Some example goals may include:

- Generate more prospect meetings
- Reduce support calls
- Speed time to demo
- Improve brand loyalty
- Answer common questions faster

2. Identify Key Features

Are you looking to dip a toe into chatbots or go all in? How much do you want to invest in chatbots today, and how important are scalability and personalization as your chat program matures? Script-based chatbots are low cost and quick to implement. You also can easily move into live chat within the same environment. For small and midmarket companies, this is usually the place to start.

3. Select a Technology Vendor

As mentioned previously, you should select a chatbot tool that either ties into your marketing and sales platform through APIs or works within your platform today. Drift is a robust chat tool that has open APIs with many other platforms. HubSpot also offers a chatbot that is natively integrated into its marketing, sales, and support tools.

4. Script Your Chats

Follow a process highly similar to the marketing workflows discussed in chapter 8 but with more branching logic. Your chatbot tool will have a planning area to map this out, or you can use a whiteboard for team collaboration. On this page is an example of a scripted chatbot sequence.

5. Set Office Hours

If you plan to use a bot and live chat hybrid approach, you need to determine the hours in which your chat option is live and identify who is on call for this purpose.

6. Push Live and Measure

Track the completion rate for each of your chatbot scripts and tweak to optimize. Be sure to look at both the hybrid and bot-only results.

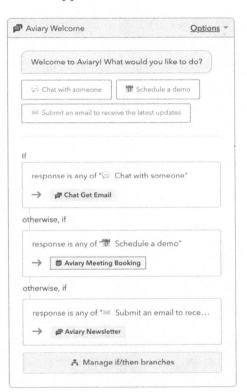

This is the backend workflow used to program the AVP Aviary chatbot. See this chatbot in action at aviaryplatform.com.

Also, inject these content types into your planning discussion and consider prioritizing them based on your level of effort versus expected use and impact. You may find sales saying "Yes!" to all these resources but not actually using them.

Sharing Content with Sales

Sometimes marketers at a company hit their stride with content, producing a wealth of new resources, and sales has no idea that these resources are available. What a missed opportunity!

Through your sales/marketing alignment team, you can discuss the best way to store content assets and make them easily consumable by sales. You also need to determine the best ways to alert sales when new resources are ready. The process for this varies by company size and organizational structure, but consider these internal sharing ideas:

1. Major Launch Training and Alerts

Whether your company is small and creating its first set of content assets or larger and launching a new solution, internal communication about the launch purpose and content pieces is critical to the success of the launch. You can communicate through meetings followed by an email with links to the content resources.

2. Monthly Marketing Updates

Using a group meeting or internal enewsletter, share new marketing resources, activities, and results. In your enewsletter, you may include a section for new content assets with links to each piece or focus on a particular business segment with all related content assets.

3. Document Management System (DMS)

With DMS technology such as Highspot, marketing staff can store content assets categorized in many ways, so sales can easily search the assets. For example, sales can find the same product datasheet in multiple categories: product line, product launch, and datasheet. Sales can also conduct metadata searches to find these assets.

Section Five

Measurement and
Return on Investment

Chapter 10
MEASURE CONTENT
MARKETING PERFORMANCE

By now, you fully appreciate the time and thought that goes into creating and executing a content-centric marketing strategy. By measuring the impact of your content marketing activities, you can learn what is working best, where to make improvements, and how your content marketing efforts are impacting your business goal successes.

This chapter guides you through definitions of key content metrics, benchmarks for those metrics, and troubleshooting tips to use when performance is below the industry standard and/or company benchmarks. We wrap up in chapter 11 with the phases of maturity associated with building a content marketing factory, and expected return on investment over time.

You need two types of measurement to effectively analyze your content marketing performance. The first is overview metrics, typically located in a color-coded dashboard or scorecard. You can gather these quickly and measure the overall health of your content marketing

Example Measurement Scorecard

Key Performance Indicator	Benchmark	Target	Q1	Q2	Q3	Q4
Achieve 20% Conversion on All Landing Pages	13%	20%	15%	19%	23%	29%
Grow New Contacts by 20% from 60 to 72/quarter	60%	72%	72%	73%	75%	76%
Grow Leads by 20% from 120 to 144/quarter	120	144	117	144	156	160
Maintain a 5% Conversion Rate on All Blog Posts	5%	5%	4%	6%	5%	4%
Grow Overall Blog Views by 15% by from 950 to 1093	950	1093	960	1000	1120	900
Grow New Blog Subscribers from by 15% from 20 to 23	20	23	21	23	24	24
Secure 25 Software Evauluation Downloads/Quarter	22	25	25	26	24	29

A measurement scorecard helps you to quickly measure the overall health of your content marketing efforts.

efforts. Define these metrics when you develop your marketing goals (see chapter 3 for a refresher).

The second type is tactical metrics, which are used to measure the effectiveness of individual activities, campaigns, or pieces of content.

This chapter explores the top five content marketing overview metrics and associated tactical metrics and presents industry benchmarks. Have your current performance metrics handy while reading this chapter. That way, you can compare your baseline performance today with the recommendations and discover how to troubleshoot when your performance is not up to par.

Web Leads

Web leads (a.k.a. form completes generated through your website) are the most interesting and important content metric to your whole organization. They represent the trust you've gained through your brand reputation, your web content, and the promise of even more engaging material (in the case of a download). They are the currency between marketing and sales. If web leads are trending downward, this is a BIG red flag, and you should take action to analyze and make improvements.

Troubleshooting tips:

- **Is web traffic also declining?** You may have an issue with SEO. Check page rankings for your top keywords to see if SERP performance has waned.

- **What is the form completion rate on individual landing pages?** If it's less than 20 percent, you have a big issue with the landing page. This could be the page content, the length of the form, or even the page design. If 40 percent or more, the page is functioning near best in class.

- **How many gated pieces of content do you have, and how dated are they?** You may need to add more gated content or refresh old assets and promote them again.

- **Are you attracting enough new contacts?** If most of your leads are existing contacts, you have an issue with awareness. Consider activities such as search optimization, events, PR, advertising, and co-marketing to expose new audiences to your brand.

Organic Search Traffic

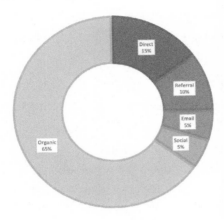

Aim to generate 65 percent or more of your web traffic through organic searches.

If you are optimizing your content and publishing content to your site on a regular basis, organic searches should generate at least 50 percent of your web traffic, and the number should be on the rise. Content marketers at best-in-class companies strive for 65 percent or more organic search traffic.

Troubleshooting tips:

- If you haven't implemented topic clusters across all major pages, including product and service family, industry, and application pages, then start with those.
- Be sure your website follows the best practices listed in chapter 8 for design, navigation, and functionality.

- Run a quick web audit with tools such as Screaming Frog to uncover gaps like security issues and broken links.
- Google Search Console and SEO Moz are also excellent SEO diagnostic tools.

Site Retention

Site retention metrics let you know whether the visitors you've attracted to your website find your content relevant and engaging. The following specific metrics measure site retention:

- **Session duration**, also known as time on-site, is pretty straightforward. You want a visitor to spend an average of two minutes or more on your site.
- **Pages per session** is another indicator that your site visitors find your site relevant and are interested enough to dig deeper. Strive for more than three pages per visit. A related metric, total pages viewed, is often used in lead scoring algorithms and by sales to separate the "somewhat interested" contacts from the "urgently seeking a solution" leads.
- **Bounce rate** represents the percentage of visitors who entered and exited your website on the same web page. This might happen if visitors clicked on search results or other links and, once they landed on your site, found the content irrelevant to their search. Strive for a bounce rate of under 60 percent.

Troubleshooting Tips:

- **Blog Metrics**: Blogs sometimes work against bounce rate. Often someone finds your outstanding blog through search, reads that blog, and leaves satisfied without venturing further into your website. Such is the nature of blogs. This is why having compelling calls to action in your blog posts is important.

- **Google Adwords**: If you're investing in Google Adwords, low site retention might be an indication that the keywords you've chosen are too broad. Try for more specific terms; you may see a drop in volume but a positive boost in quality.

- **Offers**: Review your homepage content and all other website entrance pages with a critical eye. Perhaps when visitors land on your pages, they can't immediately discern what you offer and see the benefits of your solution. Or perhaps you have an aggressive offer (think pop-up ads or "request a quote now" messages) that is a turnoff.

- **Dead Ends**: No web page should have a dead end. Include next steps or calls to action on all pages and blogs.

- **Content Depth**: Are pages that are "deep" with content keeping people engaged, or are pages with more shallow content performing better? Examine the exit rate by page on high-performing and (suspected) low-performing pages as a quantitative way to pinpoint issues in pages that are not considered valuable because they aren't converting to the next step.

- **Critical Pages**: Evaluate the individual page bounce rate of your top twenty pages. You can quickly see which pages are contributing most to the overall bounce rate and then implement the solutions listed above to those pages (e.g., call to action, etc.).

- **Measurement Tools**: If your bounce rate is crazy *low* (under 5 percent), you may have an issue with your measurement tracking code.

Email Actions and Database Health

The best measures of your email marketing initiatives are actions taken by the recipient, such as opens, click-throughs, and unsubscribes. Also highly important are measures of your database health. You need to measure your performance against industry benchmarks and performance trends over time. Note these common measures and industry benchmarks:

- **Delivery Rate**: This is the percentage of recipients whose email addresses are valid and who received your mailing. Your delivery rate should be 92 percent or higher. The opposing metric to this, the email bounce rate, is the percentage of emails that could not be delivered. The two kinds of email bounces are:

  - **Soft Email Bounce**: Email was rejected because of a reason on the recipient's end, such as a full email inbox or company security firewalls.

  - **Hard Email Bounce**: Email could not be delivered because the sender's email address was not valid. A high hard email bounce rate usually means your database is very dated or not permission-based. This can result in your company being blacklisted by your email service provider.

- **Open Rate**: This is the percentage of recipients who opened your email. Strive for a 20 percent open rate.

- **Click-Throughs**: This is the percentage of people who clicked through on a link. You can calculate it in two ways, each with its own merits:

  - **Click-Through Rate (CTR)**: The percentage of those emailed who clicked through on a link. This metric paints a picture of the overall performance of the email. Strive for a CTR of 3 percent.

  - **Click-to-Open Rate (CTOR)**: The percentage of those who opened the email compared to the percentage of those who clicked through on a link. This metric specifically indicates how well your email content performed. Aim for an 11 percent CTOR.

- **Opt-Out Rate**: This is the percentage of contacts who took action to unsubscribe from your mailings directly from the email. As you might imagine, a high opt-out rate is a red flag that either your content completely missed the mark or you are spamming a broad list of contacts who don't know you and aren't interested in your content. It could also be that you are sending your content too often and fatiguing your database.

> **If your email opt-out rate is above 5 percent, your company domain could be at risk of being blacklisted from future mailings.**

In most cases, your opt-out rate for each email should be less than 0.1 percent. The exception is for companies that have not engaged in email marketing in a while or are trying to reengage aged contacts. In those cases, you may see an opt-out rate along the lines of 1.5 to 2 percent. If your opt-out rate is above 5 percent, email services (e.g., MailChimp, Constant Contact, HubSpot, etc.) conclude that you are spamming people (rightfully so!). Those services will shut down your mailing, and your company domain could be at risk of being blacklisted from future mailings.

Troubleshooting Tips:

- **Low Deliverability Rate**: Add a step to your email workflows that puts hard bounces in a separate segment in your database, and delete these on a regular basis.

- **Low Open Rate**: Examine your subject line. It should be actionable and brief, and it should highlight key content in your enewsletter. Remember that A/B testing is a great way to analyze different types of subject lines to see which one resonates best with your audience.

- **Low Click-Through or Click-to-Open Rate**: Your recipients may believe your content lacks relevance or usefulness. To further troubleshoot, make sure that the content mentioned in the subject line is easy to locate and click on as soon as the recipient opens the email. Next, evaluate your design and content length (brevity is key). Poor design and long emails both repel many readers. Consider using a sidebar if your email or enewsletter is running long or, better yet, cut down to the most important information.

- **High Opt-Out Rate**: Examine the origin of the contacts in your database. This often indicates that the company has entered a cold list of contacts who don't know your company and are likely not a good fit (see chapter 8). Suppress these suspect contacts from your regular emails and take separate actions to either entice them to subscribe or remove them from your CRM altogether. Also consider your email frequency. You may be sending too many and repelling the very contacts you worked so hard to capture.

- **Strive to Improve All-Around**: Consider your send frequency. If your email or enewsletter cadence is infrequent or sporadic, readers are less likely to engage with you. The key is to select a frequency that you can consistently deliver on and set expectations with your readership.

Influenced Sales

With many of the integrated martech platforms, you can analyze the relationship between content, qualified leads, and closed-won business. This is powerful data because it demonstrates the ROI of your content marketing efforts and helps you determine which type of content you should create in the future.

In the following example, TREW Marketing measured lead to sale by tracking which piece of content was the very first download before someone became a customer, as indicated by landing page form completions by this group.

Chapter 11
CONTENT MARKETING RETURN ON INVESTMENT

Congratulations! You've made it to the last chapter of the book. By now you have a full understanding of what it takes to be an expert content marketer. You know how to devise, build, and execute your content marketing plans. Though you may feel excited, you probably have some questions about how much time content marketing takes and how much ROI to expect.

The Content Marketing "Factory"

In the foreword, JD Sherman compared the phases of content marketing with building and operating a factory. The factory takes time to build, but the up-front energy and costs pay off as an annuity over time, where more and more value can be extracted with each passing year.

Source: Adobe Stock

Let's take this analogy a bit further to illustrate the types of activities you should invest in each year (or each factory phase), from architectural planning and establishing processes to hitting your production stride and scaling for growth. This particular example applies well to a middle-market company that is brand new to content marketing.

Year One: Build the Content Marketing Factory

Design the Factory

- Persona development
- Brand positioning and messaging
- Content planning
- Website strategy

Establish Foundational Processes and Supporting Technology

- Marketing software
- Website redesign
- Measurement dashboard

Create Sticky Content

- Two white papers or webinars
- Four case studies
- Eight blog posts
- Corporate slide deck

Year Two: Hit Your Production Stride

Enable Sales

- Sales or marketing team alignment
- Lead flow model
- Lead scoring

Create Sticky Content

- Four white papers, ebooks, and/or webinars

- Six case studies
- Twelve technical or thought leadership blog posts
- Two to six videos
- Two visual content pieces

Publish and Promote Content

- Four landing pages
- Eight email workflows
- Twelve repurposed blog posts promoting gated material
- Weekly social media promotion
- Paid content advertising
- Quarterly enewsletter
- Ongoing web optimization

Measure and Track ROI

- Monthly results analysis
- Quarterly plan adjustment
- Annual content planning
- Annual review of personas and topic clusters

Year Three+: Scale and Accelerate Content Marketing Factory Growth

Enable Sales

- Lead pipeline model and lead scoring updates
- Buyer's journey workflows by persona
- Sales-specific content development
- Account-based content marketing

Audit, Refresh, and Repurpose Content

- Full content inventory and audit
- Historical blog optimization

- Content repurposing to new form factors
- Knowledgebase or online community forum
- Customer communication plan

Create Sticky Content

- Four white papers, ebooks, and/or webinars
- Six case studies
- Four to six leadership blog posts
- Two to six videos
- Monthly visual content

Publish and Promote Content

- Four landing pages
- Eight email workflows

Remember

- Always create content with your persona in mind
- Optimize your best-performing content again and again
- Follow a consistent content publishing cadence
- Start small by choosing one persona and one industry vertical or product to gain traction, then add other business areas over time

- Ten repurposed blog posts promoting gated material
- Weekly social media promotion
- Segmented monthly or quarterly enewsletter
- Ongoing web optimization

Measure and Track ROI

- Monthly results analysis
- Quarterly plan adjustment
- Annual content planning
- Annual review of personas and topic clusters

Buyer's Journey Stage	Key Metric
Attracting Prospects In The Discovery Phase	Visits
Engaging Visitors In The Identify Phase	Time-On-Site, Click-To-Open Rates
Gaining Trust In The Consider Phase	Leads
Solidifying Position In The Preference Phase	Revisits, Numerous Actions, Meeting Requests
Supporting Sales In The Purchase And Advocate Phases	Sales Use And Feedback

By mapping content marketing results to the buyer's journey, you can analyze and articulate business ROI.

Time to Return on Investment

In chapter 10, you learned about the key quantifiable content marketing metrics that indicate whether your activities are yielding results along the buyer's journey.

You also learned the importance of feedback from sales, not only in the form of quantitative data, such as the number of qualified leads accepted by sales, but also qualitative results ("This case study helped me win a big new contract!").

All these data points combined speak to the overall ROI of content marketing. No one-size-fits-all calculator can predict your particular company's results. Each case is unique and depends on many factors such as the abundance of content already written, the condition of your website and supporting martech stack, and the size of your marketing budget.

That being said, a 2018 ROI analysis by MIT and HubSpot showed that North American middle-market companies that adopted an inbound content marketing approach and paired it with their marketing and sales automation platform achieved these results in year 1:

- All companies increased monthly leads by two-and-a-half times or more
- More than half saw an increase in revenue
- 60 percent experienced lead quality improvement
- 70 percent increased their lead-to-customer conversion rate

TREW Marketing has seen clients perform much better than these metrics in year one, others whose second year was the swan song of content marketing, and still others fell short altogether.

These are the top nine mistakes that can tank your content marketing ROI:

1. Write for yourself (promotional) instead of your audience personas (helpful)
2. Communicate inconsistently about your company and solutions
3. Produce a low quantity of content
4. Farm out content development to writers who don't have experience communicating to technical audiences
5. Publish content on a dated website without consideration for SEO
6. Use poor grammar and punctuation
7. Stuff your content with keywords in an unauthentic manner
8. Email blast your database with irrelevant content
9. Start each prospect communication as if it were the first interaction

Take Action!

The quickest path to results is to act. With this book in hand, you have the framework and guidance you need to prepare and launch your first content marketing campaign or improve your existing inbound marketing approach. You also have data points on how content marketing improves ROI and specific ways to track progress, which can be helpful when you need to sway skeptical leadership budget holders.

Visit contentmarketingengineered.com to subscribe to my podcast on all things marketing to technical audiences. There you'll find additional helpful resources to help you get inspired and stay current on the latest trends in content marketing.

CONTENTMARKETINGENGINEERED.COM

LEARN MORE

CONTENTMARKETINGENGINEERED.COM

Subscribe to my podcast for the latest content marketing trends and advice from marketing leaders in technical companies.

Find additional helpful resources to help you get inspired and stay current on the latest trends in content marketing.

SUBSCRIBE TO THE PODCAST:
CONTENTMARKETINGENGINEERED.COM/PODCAST

References

Chapter 3

- TREW Marketing, IEEE GlobalSpec, "Smart Marketing for Engineers® 2020 Research Report," https://www.trewmarketing.com/resources-research-for-engineers.

Chapter 5

- TREW Marketing, IEEE GlobalSpec, "Smart Marketing for Engineers® 2020 Research Report," https://www.trewmarketing.com/resources-research-for-engineers.

Chapter 6

- "5 Proven Reasons to Use Visual Content in Social Media." *Smart Bird Social,* January 31, 2019, https://smartbirdsocial.net/5-reasons-use-visual-content-social-media/.
- GoToWebinar, "The 2017 Big Book of Webinar Stats," https://logmeincdn.azureedge.net/gotomeetingmedia/-/media/pdfs/gotowebinar-2017-big-book-of-webinar-stats.pdf.
- SnapApp, "What Is Interactive Content?," https://www.snapapp.com/interactive-content.
- HubSpot, Amanda Zantal-Wiener, "Why Infographics Should Be Part of Your SEO Strategy [Infographic]," October 3, 2016, https://blog.hubspot.com/marketing/infographics-for-seo-strategy?__hstc=167629729.c3ac04075b8d00f6d86e86b5b79b2b95.1559703167702.1559703167702.1559703167702.1&__hssc=167629729.1.1559703167703&__hsfp=1065685840#sm.0000e1w1nuwvbeo5sq61j1tim2kyj.
- Content Marketing Institute, Ion Interactive, Robert Rose, "The Symphony of Connected Interactive Content Marketing," April 2017, https://contentmarketinginstitute.com/wp-content/uploads/2017/06/IonInteractive_Symphony_Final.pdf.
- Venage, Nadya Khoja, "14 Visual Content Marketing Statistics to Know for 2019," https://venngage.com/blog/visual-content-marketing-statistics/.

Chapter 7

- Marko Ticak, "Quotation Marks: Rules for How to Use Them Correctly," https://www.grammarly.com/blog/quotation-marks/.

- Harald Weinreich, Hartmut Obendorf, Eelco Herder, Matthias Mayer, "Not Quite the Average: An Empirical Study of Web Use," in *ACM Transactions on the Web*, 2:1 (February 2008), article 5.

- Nielsen Norman Group, "Icon Usability," July 27, 2014, https://www.nngroup.com/articles/icon-usability/.

Chapter 8

- Trew Marketing, IEEE GlobalSpec, "Smart Marketing for Engineers® 2020 Research Report," https://www.trewmarketing.com/resources-research-for-engineers.

- Nielsen Norman Group, "Trustworthiness in Web Design: 4 Credibility Factors," May 8, 2016, https://www.nngroup.com/articles/trustworthy-design/.

- Cision, Contributor. "Global Cloud-Based Communications and PR Solutions Leader." Cision, Comms Best Practices, January 22, 2018, www.cision.com/us/2018/01/declining-attention-killing-content-marketing-strategy/. -infographics.

- Statcounter Global Stats, http://gs.statcounter.com/search-engine-market-share/all/north-america.

- Kenessey, Dee Dee de. "Why Website Personalization Will Transform Your Marketing." *HubSpot Blog,* HubSpot, November 7, 2017, https://blog.hubspot.com/customers/website-personalization-how-to.

- Allen, Olivia. "6 Stats You Should Know About Business Blogging in 2015." *HubSpot Blog,* HubSpot, November 7, 2017, https://blog.hubspot.com/marketing/business-blogging-in 2015?__hstc=191390709.336e0349d2d51236c11c3d51ad606 3ae.1492011740788.1492011740788.1494862983488.2&__hssc=19139 0709.1.1494862983488&__hsfp=1283505112.

- Mitra, Achinta. "The Importance of Industrial Email Marketing for Targeting Engineers." *Industrial Marketing Today,* Industrial Marketing

Blog, April 22, 2019, www.industrialmarketingtoday.com/the-importance-of-industrial-email-marketing-for-targeting-engineers/.

- Tony Haile, "What You Think You Know About the Web Is Wrong," March 9, 2014, https://time.com/12933/what-you-think-you-know-about-the-web-is-wrong/.
- Alphametic, Matthew Capala, "Global Search Engine Market Share for 2018 in the Top 15 GDP Nations," https://alphametic.com/global-search-engine-market-share.
- Everage, Researchscape International, "2019 Trends in Personalization," https://www.evergage.com/resources/ebooks/trends-in-personalization-survey-report/.

Chapter 9

- Trew Marketing, IEEE GlobalSpec, "Smart Marketing for Engineers® 2020 Research Report," https://www.trewmarketing.com/resources-research-for-engineers.
- Content Marketing Institute, MarketingProfs, "B2B Content Marketing 2019 Benchmarks, Budgets, and Trends - North America," https://contentmarketinginstitute.com/wp-content/uploads/2018/10/2019_B2B_Research_Final.pdf.
- Sender Score, "Return Path," https://www.senderscore.org/.
- The Business of Events, "Learning with TBOE," February 5, 2019, https://www.thebusinessofevents.com.au/how-to-improve-your-brand-perception-through-an-event/.
- LinkedIn, "Ad Targeting Best Practices," https://business.linkedin.com/marketing-solutions/success/best-practices/ad-targeting-best-practices.

Chapter 10

- Trew Marketing, IEEE GlobalSpec, "Smart Marketing for Engineers® 2020 Research Report," https://www.trewmarketing.com/resources-research-for-engineers.
- Demand Metric, "The State of Video Marketing 2018," https://www.vidyard.com/resources/the-state-of-video-marketing-in-2018-demand-metric-report/#nav-top.

- Inc, David Finkel, "7 Tactics Guaranteed to Increase Your Conversion Rate," November 9, 2016, https://www.inc.com/david-finkel/7-tactics-guaranteed-to-increase-your-conversion-rate.html.

- Business Insider Intelligence, "80% of Businesses Want Chatbots by 2020," December 14, 2016, https://www.businessinsider.com/80-of-businesses-want-chatbots-by-2020-2016-12.

- Spiceworks, "Spiceworks Study Reveals 40 Percent of Large Businesses Will Implement Intelligent Assistants or Chatbots by 2019," April 2, 2018, https://www.spiceworks.com/press/releases/spiceworks-study-reveals-40-percent-large-businesses-will-implement-intelligent-assistants-chatbots-2019/.

- Comm100, "Millennials Prefer Live Chat for Speed and Convenience," https://www.comm100.com/resources/infographic/millennials-prefer-live-chat-speed-convenience/.

Chapter 11

- HubSpot, "The 2018 HubSpot Growth Platform ROI Report," https://www.hubspot.com/roi.

About the Author

Wendy Covey is a CEO, technical marketing leader, and one of *The Wall Street Journal's* 10 Most Innovative Entrepreneurs in America. She also holds a Texas fishing record.

Over the last 20 years, Wendy has helped hundreds of technical companies build trust and fill their sales pipelines using compelling technical content. Her company, TREW Marketing, is a full-service marketing agency that helps clients connect with customers, build trust, and drive sustainable results using a proven content marketing approach.

Through TREW Marketing, Wendy conducts large-scale surveys of engineers and technical professionals to better understand how they find information, gain trust in brands, and make purchase decisions. This research allows marketers to better target their efforts to build trust and generate demand with technical buyers.

As a speaker, Wendy educates audiences in technical storytelling, content planning, and development throughout the buyer's journey, working effectively with sales and measuring marketing ROI.

Acknowledgments

As a business leader, you quickly learn that you are only as good as the team you surround yourself with. It is no different when it comes to writing a book. *Content Marketing, Engineered* was a highly collaborative project. I pulled in the best of the TREW Crew and TREW friends to lend their expertise, critical eye, and creativity throughout the writing and design process.

Morgan Norris, TREW brand strategist, lead writer, and longest-standing member of the TREW Crew, played a crucial role in the formation of the book. Her expertise in branding and crazy skills at writing excellent technical content are imprinted in every chapter. Thank you, Morgan, for your enthusiastic embrace of this project and for sharing your wisdom with both me and the readers.

Sarah Seward, TREW inbound marketing specialist and imagery whiz, was another close collaborator. She had a vision for how much of the book material could be communicated with imagery, much in the way she works every day to attract attention to TREW Marketing's content through her graphics work.

Laura Lee, TREW creative designer, came back for an encore performance, this being the second book by a TREW Marketing author that she's designed. Her creativity and eye for continuity were the perfect match for this project.

Lee Chapman, Jennifer Dawkins, and Erin Gleeson ensured that the advice and best practices I provided were true to what is producing results with the TREW Marketing clients they manage. From content planning to the exact way in which email opens are measured, their attention to detail strengthened this book greatly. Abby Dowden jumped in wearing many different hats, including citations, book promotion, and sales. TREW friends Stephanie Logeret and Johanna Franke put on their well-worn editorial hats to ensure accuracy, sound writing, and compelling prose.

The top-notch publishing team at Greenleaf wore many hats, from project manager to editor and design consultant. Best of all, they held my work to the highest standard, ensuring that the quality of *Content Marketing, Engineered* rates among that of the bestsellers of the business publishing world.

Throughout the book you see examples of work, the vast majority of which originated from TREW Marketing's client collaboration. We build tight relationships with our client partners, and we appreciate their permission to share specific examples so that the lessons in this book are easier to understand and remember.

TREW Marketing's relationship with HubSpot, a market-leading business software company, dates back almost a decade. In that time, we've seen HubSpot remain fiercely committed to their partner channel, providing support in countless ways to TREW's business growth. I've been honored to serve on their Partner Advisory Committee and have made many friends along the way.

Thank you to JD Sherman, COO of HubSpot, for providing the book foreword. When I first met JD, I learned of his background in the semiconductor industry, and we shared some chuckles over our shared challenges of working inside a highly technical environment in a business role. Over the years JD and I have kept up with each other's ups and downs, including our annual bet on the Texas A&M versus LSU football game. Despite his Tigers background, I knew that he would be the perfect person to introduce this book.

I'd also like to recognize advance readers: Eric Starkloff, National Instruments; Titus Crabb, Vertech; Jose Rivera, Control System Integrators Association; and Josh Doty, ANSYS. Your endorsement of the book means a great deal to me.

This book quickly turned into a family affair. My husband Randy, an experienced technical sales manager, provided candid feedback on his experiences of when marketing truly makes a positive impact and when it does more harm (or distraction) than good. Even the Covey teenagers pitched in with the book—Lauren and Grayson worked on citations and book publishing logistics.

This has been a family collaboration in a different sense, too. My school counselor Mom and civil-engineer-professional-turned-college-professor Dad both had a gift for inspiring students to discover their passions, balanced with the practical steps necessary to turn dreams into reality. I try to wear both of these visionary and integrator hats in my day-to-day work leading the agency and working with new clients. I hope that this balance comes across in this book.

And finally, a very special thank you to TREW co-founder and forth-coming content marketing textbook author Rebecca Geier, whose vision of TREW Marketing's role as educator to the technical marketing community led to the very existence of the book in your hands. *Content Marketing, Engineered* is at heart a deeper dive into many of the topics included in Rebecca's debut book, *Smart Marketing for Engineers: An Inbound Marketing Guide to Reaching Technical Audiences.*

Thank you for your time, reader. I look forward to your visit at contentmarketingengineered.com.

Index